"Bridget Gee approaches this crucial top[ic with] wise biblical insights, and one-of-a-kind humor. I have been married for thirty years, and her book helped me want to have a more tender relationship with God, so I guess this is for everyone! Read this book, and you just might learn to be a better friend and how to get closer to God."

Doug Schaupp, national director of evangelism with InterVarsity Christian Fellowship/USA and coauthor of *Breaking the Huddle*

"Approachable and winsome, Bridget's story is a welcome reminder that—contrary to popular belief—singleness is not a disease in need of remedy. My own journey has been vastly different from Bridget's in many ways, yet the core truth of our experience remains so much the same: no matter how we arrive at singleness or why we stay here, the same God is ready to meet us in our holy aloneness and take great delight in us."

Gregory Coles, author of *Single, Gay, Christian* and *No Longer Strangers*

"In this winsome and confessional book, Bridget challenges the ways Christians conflate singleness with waiting. Instead, Bridget invites readers into a pilgrimage where we discover love, silliness, fullness, delight, connection, and even loss and loneliness as a context for life with God. This story leads all of us to a deeper and more humanizing vision of discipleship."

Jason Gaboury, author of *Wait with Me: Meeting God in Loneliness*

"In *Single, Just Because*, Bridget Gee offers a refreshing, relatable, honest, and insightful exploration of the joys and struggles of singleness. Far from being a manual on preparing for what's next, Gee focuses on what's now and how to live fully and faithfully in the tension of longing and contentment. *Single, Just Because* invites all singles into the richness of God, community, and holy aloneness, and out of self-doubt, distrust, and loneliness."

Alicia Akins, author of *Invitations to Abundance*

"Very few of us have ever wanted to be 'the singleness gal,' as Bridget Gee puts it. As Gee freely admits, she didn't want to be either. But the grace, patience, and insight that God has given her through her experiences with singleness shine through her story, offering a helpful light to others on the same path."

Gina Dalfonzo, author of *One by One: Welcoming the Singles in Your Church*

"Profound and funny, spiritual yet irreverent, Bridget Gee deals with the universal themes of longing, friendship, intimacy, and making peace with ourselves. This is not so much a book on singleness as it is on what it means to be human. *Single, Just Because* sets us on a journey with the author of finding her true self in the midst of pain and loneliness. With hilarious wit and remarkable vulnerability, this book will call all readers—whether single, married, celibate, or sexually active—into a deeper understanding of true intimacy."

Scott Bessenecker, director of global engagement and justice, InterVarsity Christian Fellowship/USA

"In a world where many travel in pairs, it is easy to believe that journeying solo is less than ideal. In her insightful book, *Single, Just Because*, Bridget Gee invites us to accompany her on a transformative pilgrimage to discover our true worth rooted in the glorious image of God, not in our marital status. The path may be challenging, as the painful realities of loneliness and disappointment appear, but keep traveling. You will encounter an abundance of hope and healing through Scripture, prayers, and authentic stories filled with wisdom. Whether you are single or married, you will enjoy this book as you are reminded of God's faithful character, redemptive power, and the deep love he has for each one of us."

Christine Wagoner, author of *Finding Your Yes*

SINGLE. JUST BECAUSE

A PILGRIMAGE INTO HOLY ALONENESS

BRIDGET GEE

An imprint of InterVarsity Press
Downers Grove, Illinois

InterVarsity Press
P.O. Box 1400 | Downers Grove, IL 60515-1426
ivpress.com | email@ivpress.com

InterVarsity Press® is the publishing division of InterVarsity Christian Fellowship/USA®. For more information, visit intervarsity.org.

All Scripture quotations, unless otherwise indicated, are taken from The Holy Bible, New International Version®, NIV®. Copyright © 1973, 1978, 1984, 2011 by Biblica, Inc.™ Used by permission of Zondervan. All rights reserved worldwide. www.zondervan.com. The "NIV" and "New International Version" are trademarks registered in the United States Patent and Trademark Office by Biblica, Inc.™

While any stories in this book are true, some names and identifying information may have been changed to protect the privacy of individuals.

The publisher cannot verify the accuracy or functionality of website URLs used in this book beyond the date of publication.

Cover design and image composite: David Fassett
Interior design: Jeanna Wiggins

ISBN 978-1-5140-0478-4 (print) | ISBN 978-1-5140-0479-1 (digital)

Printed in the United States of America ♾

Library of Congress Cataloging-in-Publication Data
A catalog record for this book is available from the Library of Congress.

29 28 27 26 25 24 23 22 | 8 7 6 5 4 3 2 1

For Dad,

*who introduced me
to the Love of my life*

And for Mom,

*who has shown me
how to love*

CONTENTS

Introduction

AN INVITATION INTO PILGRIMAGE

This isn't the book you're expecting, I promise you that now. Rather than offer you a self-help guide or a comprehensive theology of singleness, I offer you my story. I am not an expert in much, other than in being single. I'm very good at that. I can't give you all the answers or speak to subjects on which I have little authority. What I can do though, is create space for us.

I am inviting you on a pilgrimage into holy aloneness. In recent years, pilgrimage has become a wonderful tool of spiritual formation for me. It's helped me look at my life differently and practice a deeper and more profound faith in God. I'll be using pilgrimage to frame the way I talk about singleness throughout this book. You may be more familiar with your own singleness than you are with pilgrimage, and that's okay. I am too.

Let's start by getting on the same page. My working definition of pilgrimage is *a journey to a destination, usually in the footsteps of others, to return to a place you belong.*

I don't believe the destination of singleness is marriage, contrary to everything we've been told in and outside of the church. I think the journey of singleness leads deeper into God's presence, or what I like to call "holy aloneness"—the place where you are wholly known, wholly seen, and wholly loved by your Creator. That's the place we all belong.

Pilgrimage happens in so many of our favorite movies and stories: *The Odyssey, The Lord of the Rings, The Wizard of Oz,* and all over the Bible, just to name a few.

Consider one of the most famous pilgrimages, the escape of Moses and the Israelites from Egypt and their forty years of wandering in the desert. Early on their journey, Moses has a holy moment alone with God in the middle of the mountains: "And he passed in front of Moses, proclaiming, 'The LORD, the LORD, the compassionate and gracious God, slow to anger, abounding in love and faithfulness'" (Exodus 34:6).

This claim God makes about his character is repeated throughout the Bible—in Psalms, Joel, and Jonah for example. For generations, the Israelites remembered who God showed himself to be on that original pilgrimage into the Promised Land. God proved his character over and over, in all the highs and lows with his people. He never changed.

In my own story, my own pilgrimage into holy aloneness, God has shown himself to be merciful and gracious, slow to anger, and abounding in steadfast love for me too. At times he has had to invite me up to a mountain alone to do it. While this is a journey of aloneness in a relationship-oriented world, we're never truly alone—God goes with us himself, with his promise to walk with us, and the truth that he walked this life before us.

These truths might be the start and finish of where my story and yours overlap. God is the same and has the same promises and invitations into his presence for us both. After that, it's likely that our pilgrimages look wildly different. Nonetheless, we are pilgrims together. I want to make space for you, especially if your singleness has been different from mine.

You should know some things about me before we begin.

My singleness happens to be in a Western, evangelical, heteronormative context. I am an upper-middle-class, White, thirty-something-year-old, cisgender, straight woman. I've never been married or engaged, and, for the cherry on top of my singleness sundae, I'm a virgin too. I like to joke that I'm a dime a dozen, in that there are plenty of women *just* like me. But it's true—they are funny, smart, educated, well-resourced, think similar things, live similar lives. I check all the boxes that my evangelical bubble wants me to, but I have grown weary of this bubble. I've needed to say yes to a pilgrimage beyond my context.

I know there are many of you out there, my fellow pilgrims, who have different stories and backgrounds. I want to honor that. Let the parts of my story that relate to you speak to your life and heart, and ditch the rest. It's okay. Our journeys are different. My life is not prescriptive.

If your singleness is much younger, praise God. If yours is singleness after loss, death, or divorce, you are loved and welcome here. If your singleness doesn't include virginity, know that it's not less valid. Perhaps your singleness is much older than mine. God bless you.

I hope that some of your singleness out there is male singleness and BIPOC singleness and all types of queer singleness. And I hope my story is a blessing to you too. I hope some parts resonate deeply.

But your story is your own!

Your story is beautiful and important, and likely uniquely challenging. My singleness has privilege attached to it, which at times makes it a really comfortable singleness. There are so many ways I don't have to struggle in my singleness because of the privilege given to my sexuality, gender identity, and race.

Although many hurdles may be found along the path of singleness, I cannot speak to all of them in this book. I simply share my story and offer some ways for us to step closer to our Creator. It's all I can do here.

As you sit with me in my story, I encourage you to think of yours. Your story matters. You'll notice repeating themes throughout this book—those I needed to learn over and over until they sunk in. Learning about God's mercy, grace, patience, and love is still central to my daily life. I pray now that Jesus will show his mercy, grace, patience, and steadfast love in your life too.

In addition to sharing about my life, each chapter includes a "pilgrimage moment." These are opportunities for you to pause before moving forward in the text. Pilgrimage is an ancient contemplative practice that's been around for generations. Some of the pilgrimage moments are based in other contemplative practices of old. My hope is that they give you practical steps into the presence of God, to journey more fully with him in your singleness.

Have a blessed journey.

1

SINGLENESS IS NOT THE PROBLEM

"So, Morgan, what was your response tonight?"

We were sitting outside the student union on a late-September evening after our weekly gathering. Morgan was a new freshman whose parents had met in our InterVarsity Christian Fellowship chapter in the 1990s. She was eighteen. Truly fresh. I had just given a talk and invited the students to respond by writing down a burden they needed to lay at the foot of the cross. We set up a foam cross for students to tack them to.

"Well, I was thinking about my singleness," Morgan said.

"Really? Why's that?" I asked, curious because I hadn't mentioned relationships in my talk that night.

"I'm just so afraid that I won't meet my husband. What if I don't? And I know, I'm young, everyone says that, but it's just a worry that I have to keep giving to Jesus."

I smiled. "That's fair, Morgan. I'm glad you felt like you could do that tonight. But I do want to reassure you. You have your whole life ahead of you. You're eighteen and so beautiful. You will absolutely find love. I'm sure of it."

"I know, I know, but it's just . . . what if I don't?"

"What *if* you don't? I'm twenty-seven and I haven't found love—"

"Exactly! And my heart breaks for you!" She interrupted my point.

I threw my head back in laughter. "Don't waste your heartbreak on me, babe! I'm twenty-seven and single and I'm happy with how my life is—I don't look at all these years as less beautiful or valid since romance hasn't been center stage. Life is so much more than finding love in one person. You were right to lay down that worry, tonight. I have to lay it down all the time. But rest assured, I am not heartbroken. Not right now anyway."

Morgan will never know twenty-seven-year-old singleness. She did in fact meet her husband in our chapter, just like her parents. Her now-husband, Carson, was another one of my students; he was not overly concerned about his own singleness, but ended up being a huge blessing to Morgan and her family. They got together only a year after the family lost Morgan's dad. I see God's handiwork in their relationship. God was kind to connect her with a partner even before her freshman year ended. Her story is different from mine. She endured only a few months of adult singleness, whereas mine has lasted a decade and change.

People show undue concern all the time for my now thirty-something singleness.

"How are you still single, Bridget?"

"How is it that you have not been snatched up yet?"

"It's an injustice that you're not married."

"Your husband is going to be so lucky."

Usually, I'm having a wonderful conversation about life and God when I hear these sentiments from the mouths of my friends. I don't always know how to respond. Sometimes I feel uncomfortable, sometimes I feel flattered. After years of hearing such things, a narrative has risen to the surface:

It is somehow wrong for me to be single.

I know that the truth of the matter is that my friends and family are experiencing a moment of delight in me when they say things like this; they actually mean to tell me they feel loved by me and find me incredibly lovable. And I write that without a hint of irony—I mean it. This is the most common response I get when people in my life are amazed by me and feel big feelings of love for me. They wish that I was regularly loved and appreciated by a spouse.

But I'm not.

In fact, I've been single for over a decade—and not for lack of trying, believe me. This fact often shocks people during bonding moments we share. They wonder how could I have gone so long without being chosen by a man?

And so, in that moment, rather than affirming and encouraging me for who I am, they feel confused that I'm still single, and they want me to answer for it. The confusion seems to suggest that my personhood is going to waste by not being in a romantic relationship.

To be honest, I've felt this way too at times when singleness makes me ache.

I'm not held enough.

I'm not told I'm beautiful nearly enough, in my humble opinion.

I rarely have anyone offer to make me a meal.

Days can pass without anyone checking in on my well-being or encouraging me to keep going.

I get to structure my life around me and me alone, which can be a bit unmooring.

And I agree that it is wild that I have yet to meet a man who wants to spend the rest of his life with me.

While all those things are true, it's a lie to believe that my personhood is wasted just because I'm not being loved by a partner. In American culture, marriage is often discussed as a checkpoint in life, a sure thing. That sense of entitlement to marriage turns singleness into a problem, a curse, or a burden. But this mindset only makes sense when you're looking through a lens that centers romantic relationships.

When we talk about singleness, dating, and marriage this way, it can be dehumanizing. We are wholly valuable regardless of our relationships, our accomplishments, or our lovability for that matter.

Dealing with my own singleness has been challenging enough without the consistent questioning from others. For most of my adulthood, I've treated myself with contempt because of my singleness. It's only in the last couple years that I've been able to stop treating it like a curse and start peeling back the layers to understand who I am and how I got here. I'm single not because there's something wrong with me or anyone else. I'm single just because. That's how it's worked out so far. I won't blame anything or anyone but God and his mercy, because even though I cringe at calling it a "gift," I know that God is not uncomfortable with my singleness. He knows what's going on, even when I don't.

A few years ago, when I became restless with having such a negative view of my relationship status, I decided to work on actively embracing it. I wanted to learn to trust God more with my life, and I thought it was time to unpack the intricacies of my singleness—what parts I have control over, what spiritual aspects are at play, and what value systems perpetuate my struggles. I was met with both encouragement and discomfort while seeking out answers and healthier conversations around singleness. Some of my friends felt this change in me was a breath of fresh air; others said I was defining myself too much by my relationship status. But that's exactly what I had been doing before this move in a healthier direction. I was convinced that society's judgment was right, that my partnerless, sexless life was less than valuable.

Society loves to center romantic pairing, love stories, and getting married—it's a literary and historic reality. Traditionally, comedies are meant to end in weddings with the main characters living happily ever after. These days, most movies and TV shows include a romantic plot line in order to draw an audience. In many cultures, marriage is the final step into adulthood—a real coming of age, a solidifying of purpose and value.

From a young age we are overtly and subliminally encouraged to attain opposite-sex relationships, in which our identities make sense to everyone else and our lives seem stable behind the white picket fence of the American Dream (or something like it). We are sold one version of what life can be—packaged, boxed up, and limited. We are told that all the good stuff happens within that box, that it's where all the fun and value is found.

As I become more comfortable with my own singleness, I rage against that box. I am bored by the story that I'm offered as a single person. Instead of being married by twenty-seven, like I imagined I might be, I became the Singleness Gal™ (just kidding, I haven't trademarked it . . . yet). I hold the tension of wanting to be married with the knowledge that marriage isn't all there is to life.

I've always been drawn to living a different kind of life, imagined for me by the stories of the kingdom of God.

Scripture doesn't center human love stories. They are in the Bible no doubt, but that's not what the Bible is about. It's not even about human marriage. It's not about human reproduction. The story of Scripture is about a covenant relationship between humankind and its Creator. It's about reproducing eternal life. It's about being invited into the family of God as an heir to the kingdom. If you follow The Way, then you do not believe in a book of romantic fairy tales. You believe in the real deal of what life is all about. That's why I am baffled when the church sounds more like the world than the Word.

THE REAL PROBLEM

One afternoon early in my ministry career, I sat in a coffee shop booth with my coworker and good friend Chris. Before we got down to business, he made a surprising admission.

"Bridget, your singleness has seriously opened my eyes." Although he was only six months my senior, he had been married since his sophomore year in college.

"Oh yeah?" I asked curiously and cautiously, bracing myself for what he might say next.

"Yeah. I was at my dad's church last weekend for a men's retreat, and I couldn't help but notice that all the content was geared toward husbands and fathers. Like, they just expected that we were all married with children."

"Were there any single guys there?" I asked.

"Oh yeah, definitely, but it was the first time I realized that the content wasn't for everyone in the room."

"It's as if the expectation is that those single men will one day be husbands and fathers, so it will eventually apply to them, right?"

"Yes! Exactly!"

"And how did that make you feel as a married man in the room?" I asked.

"Well, I felt a little ruined! I wouldn't have noticed it had I not been exposed to your perspective as a single person. And it just sucks because getting married and having kids is no guarantee."

How sweet that moment was for me, a hopeless romantic who was hopelessly single and whose friends were marrying left and right. Finally, one of them recognized what I see all the time in churches and in the content put out by Christian leadership.

And that's that it often lacks imagination.

It often lacks a dreamer's perspective and vision for what our lives can look like. These conferences, sermons, and devotionals encourage lifestyles that look more like the Western cultural ideal than the wild, upside-down, and unconventional kingdom of God.

In campus ministry, our aim is not to create an army of future husbands, wives, fathers, and mothers out of the young singles we work with, but instead to develop disciples of Jesus. To develop world changers here and now! They may eventually become husbands and wives, fathers and mothers, but we do not prepare them for something not guaranteed. We prepare them for the sure thing: Jesus' eternal reign and our partnership with him as coheirs in the kingdom of God.

There needs to be a new wave of discipleship in singleness in our current cultural climate.

During my adulthood, things have been changing in the United States. The average age of first marriage has risen by years instead of months. It seems the longer I'm single, the closer that number gets to my age. Single people now make up a little over half of the adult population.

And yet, in the evangelical movement one can graduate high school with a deep theological grasp of traditional Christian marriage yet hardly have a robust understanding of what it means to be a part of the global church or even a grasp of engaging with God in their personal life. We've spent too much time on marriage discipleship for single people.

When the church and popular culture say the same thing about singleness, we have a major problem.

I get it. Marriage books, conferences, and materials exist to help marriages *last*, not to convince people to get married. But being hyper-focused on marriage leads many singles to believe they are missing something vital to abundant life.

LOCKED AWAY IN A TOWER

Disney's *Tangled* is a telling of the fairy tale of Rapunzel, the princess with long flowing hair, locked away in a tower. It's one of my favorites of all the Disney movies. I first saw it in theaters with my little brother Luke when I was twenty and he was just thirteen. It made me very emotional, but I tried so hard to hide my sappiness from him that only one tear escaped my left tear duct while he sat on my right. I don't know why I was so eager to hide my emotions because as we drove home, I confessed them to him, and we had a good laugh. Now I openly weep when the movie makes me emotional.

The movie's opening number shows a grown-up Rapunzel singing about her daily schedule—all the things she does locked away in the tower all day. After listing off her chores and hobbies, she sings, "Stuck in the same place I've always been, I'll keep wonderin', and wonderin'... When will my life begin?"

All Rapunzel wants is to leave her tower on her birthday to see up close the annual display of stars she's always admired from a distance. But her captor (pretending to be her mother) makes the excuse that the world out there is too dangerous for her, and so she traps her year after year.

There have been so many days I've felt like Rapunzel—trapped in my singleness, wondering and wondering and wondering and wondering when will *my* life begin? As if my life would begin when I was finally chosen by a man and I was finally in a marriage. The world of love, purpose, fun, and freedom wasn't for me if I wasn't married. That's what I had heard from the world and the church.

But deep down, I didn't buy it. Couldn't I be enough just being me? Couldn't I have a full and beautiful life as a single person? Couldn't we stop believing and acting like being in a relationship or a marriage unlocks some kind of magical portal to a better life?

Too often, the answers we give each other for our deep hurts and longings are romance, dating, love, and marriage. None of these things are inherently bad, but they are not lasting answers to the problems in our souls. We need to find better ones—there's a whole creation out there that God gave us to interact with and delight in.

Rapunzel's desire to venture beyond her tower is so right on; she was right to imagine more for her life. It isn't until she meets the film's other main character, Flynn Rider, that she finds out the stars are actually lanterns in a festival that the king and queen put on for their lost princess on her birthday each year.

When Rapunzel and Flynn finally get to the festival and sing *Tangled*'s key musical number, I completely lose it. As they float on a boat outside the palace, lanterns start to ascend into the night sky all around them and they sing, "I See the Light."

"Standing here it's all so clear / I'm where I'm meant to be / And at last, I see the light."

Rapunzel is finally getting what she wants: to see the lanterns up close. She doesn't yet know they've been for her all along! Her parents never gave up on her return.

That first time I let the song and scene sink into my soul, I turned into mush at the thought of my Father. The King who waits and waits and sends out endless signs and light in the hope that his children will return to him. God wants us to have that same moment that Rapunzel has in the boat—the fog lifted, our worlds shifted, finally seeing him.

Tangled is not primarily a love story. It's a pilgrimage. Rapunzel leaves behind the comfort of life as she knows it for a new experience. Along the way, she finds out that life has more to offer her than she could imagine. *Tangled* is a story of returning to who you are, finding out what life is really about, dreaming dreams, taking risks, and opening your eyes to the invitations left for you.

Rapunzel's story is my story. It's our story. We aren't locked away in towers of single loneliness, but we may be missing out on real life with Jesus because of the false stories we've been told. We can venture out into all that life has to offer. We can open our eyes to the ways God beckons us into his kingdom, into his family, and into our positions as his royal ones.

Jesus says in John 10:10 (ESV), "The thief comes only to steal and kill and destroy. I came that they may have life and have it abundantly."

He offers all of us abundant life. That doesn't mean a married life. That doesn't even mean an easy and happy life. But it does mean a life that is full and free, with unwavering peace from God and constant access to joy unspeakable. Unconditionally, God's promises are available to us. We don't have to be married for that to be true.

But we do have to be willing to leave behind the lies we've been told and to seek out real life in Jesus. What are the stories you've been told that hold you captive to a limited life? What are the realities at play that keep you thinking that your singleness is less than God's best for you?

MOVING FROM STARVATION OR GLUTTONY TO HEALTH

Sometimes you go through seasons of loving life, hardly thinking about your singleness. And then other times, it's all you can think about. The truth is that singleness does define us in some seasons. We live in the tension of hating being alone—alone in our households, alone in our hurts and sadness and struggles—but loving the freedom and joy that singleness affords us at the same time.

We long for companionship. There is nothing wrong with this.

We long to be touched. Biological realities are at work in us, making this absolutely normal.

We long to be championed in our goals and dreams.

We long to be seen and understood because we want to validate our existence.

In a lot of ways, a romantic relationship *can* provide all these things. But that's a tower we get trapped in: we wrap up the solution for all our longings in this one place.

What if, as in my case, it just keeps not working out? As much as I've tried, I haven't been able to land a long-term romantic relationship.

Does that mean I go without my longings being met?

Some of us deprive ourselves of what we want and need when it doesn't come in the package we expect. Others go out and get it by any means necessary. Both approaches are commonplace, but both only cause more strife. The first requires us to see ourselves as robots with a specific set of instructions for meeting our needs. The second requires us to see others as the means of getting our needs met. Where did this come from? I think the church encourages starvation and the world encourages gluttony. What an inhumane tension to live in! There must be a better way.

Throughout this book, we will explore a healthier approach to the longings and needs that arise in singleness.

We are made for companionship, connection, romance, love, and commitment. Relationships are supposed to be beautiful and fulfilling, to bring us joy, life, and wholeness. However, there's a lot of brokenness, abuse, and unhealth in our relationships. A lot of us are living without the love and connection we are made for—romantic or otherwise.

So how do I go about getting that when time and time again, romantic relationships are not working out for me? How do I treat my longings with grace and kindness, and a bit of wisdom?

What we do with our longings is a great measure of our character and maturity.

I applaud people who go after what they want unapologetically, full force. I love seeing people ditch societal expectations to fully embrace who they are and what they've been made to do. It's inspiring. I think we all love those stories to some extent, but the status quo of the church and the world pulls us back in over and over.

One of the biggest reasons I am grateful to be part of the kingdom of God is that it beats every human system. Every human-made construct eventually crumbles. And praise God for that! That's his mercy. All the things we think we want and need become incredibly dull next to Jesus and the life he offers. Jesus has living water for us—overflowing, bubbling up. His life for us doesn't ever end (John 4)!

The cost of following Jesus is high, however (Luke 9:23). And sometimes that means giving up a version of yourself meant to please others. Or giving up a version of your life you've come up with yourself. Either way, following Jesus means real freedom. Life with Jesus means you always have access to your Creator and that you reflect him with every inhale and exhale.

My aim in this book is to help you envision an abundant life, one that you are called to by Jesus, no matter your relationship status. Throughout my story, I share how Jesus has crushed the lies of the world and flipped anti-kingdom structures on their heads in my life. In my pilgrimage, God has helped me see how different and better his invitations are for me than those found elsewhere.

Let's be like Rapunzel and leave our towers behind to discover true Life.

Pilgrimage Moment: Take the First Step

Are you ready for our first pilgrimage moment together?

Actually, that's my main question for you: Are you ready to move in a new direction with your singleness? Maybe it's your attitude that needs some change. Maybe you need an overhaul of your view and beliefs around your singleness as a follower of Jesus. Maybe you need to wrestle with God for a while over some things. No matter how you're coming in, this likely will be a healing journey for you.

Take a moment before moving on, and consider where you've been and what brought you here. How's the journey been so far? Is there something you need from God in order to take the first step on your pilgrimage into holy aloneness?

Ask him for it!

The pilgrimage began when you picked up this book. I'm excited for you.

2

THE MOST ROMANTIC ONE

God ruined my first kiss.

No really, I mean it.

I've been a romantic for as long as I can remember. In pre-kindergarten, I wrote my schoolyard crush a cute love note and left it in his cubby, hoping he would reciprocate. I can't remember how he responded, but I was five. I don't think I expected much. I've made a habit of shooting my shot with my crushes all my life. I don't know what it is—perhaps the weight of my feelings becomes too much for my heart to bear that I feel I must get it off my chest. And even though I've been shot down time and time again, the hope in my heart remains. I keep trying.

In middle school, I had the biggest crush of my life. So big that my homeroom teacher knew about it and offered to send me to his classroom for a "study period" so I could stare at him. I foolishly never took her up on that offer. He was the only reason I wanted to go to the school dances. To creep on him and dream up alternate realities. To feel the rush of romantic possibilities as a thirteen-year-old in a dimly lit cafeteria. Completely innocent. Completely normal. But as a child of a former drug addict turned born-again Christian, the dance wasn't going to happen. We didn't even listen to *secular music* at home. So I had to live with all my pent-up feelings the best way I knew how—I opened a file on our family desktop computer and started to write letters to my future husband. I wanted to let him know about my crush, even if it didn't end up being him. (It hasn't. So far. I mean, you never know, right?)

This is just how romantic I am. The way I've functioned in the world has always been with wide eyes filled with wonder, head in the clouds, looking for love. The irony of it all is that for someone so romantic, so fixated on love, I hardly ever got any romantic attention. I wasn't asked out on a legit date until college. I was never taken to prom. I never had a romantic valentine.

One year in high school, I woke up before sunrise to leave flowers and carefully curated mixtapes of love songs at my friends' houses on February 14. So even though I never really had a lot going for me romantically, I created moments of splendor, love, and delight. Romance is simply about the mystery and excitement of life. Seeing, feeling, and experiencing the fullness of it rather than staying complacent. I had survived my singleness this way for years.

Don't get me wrong, there were a lot of "almost" moments. Mutual crushes, pseudo-dates, chemistry, flirtation, and emotionally tense moments that ultimately turned into nothing. They remained as plot points in journals, or in those letters to my future husband, or in drawn-out phone conversations with my best friend Felicia on the landline after school. All these almost moments could have become romantic milestones in my life, but it wasn't until my sophomore year in college that I had my first boyfriend and my first kiss.

Sophomore year was the first year I lived in my own apartment. It felt like the first real year of being an adult. And

I loved it. I was thriving. I lived on the edge of campus and had a part-time job nearby; my friends all lived in the same complex or in the next one over, and we were all in InterVarsity Christian Fellowship together, having a blast. Sharing life, community, and Jesus. It was a marvelous year. I remember one afternoon riding my bike home and just telling God, "I am so happy."

I felt utterly content. I had no need.

And then Cupid struck.

I had been trying to get the attention of one guy by flirting with another and ended up on an accidental date with the latter rather than the former. On a mid-February afternoon, I hung out with my college besties and told them I didn't want to have the date later that night. I was happy. I had no need for a man's attention—especially one whose attention I didn't particularly want. They told me that was okay, it didn't have to be a date—just enjoy myself.

Brandon and I had a great time. We laughed, we played Boggle, we talked about serious stuff and then laughed some more. Before we knew it, it was after midnight. The clock struck February 14, and uh oh, I caught feelings for the decoy guy. Before long, I was knee-deep in my first-ever official romantic relationship.

It would be safe to assume that I proceeded to lose myself in the throes of love, but the opposite was true. I became incredibly practical and serious amid my newfound romance. I even tried to convince Brandon that we should break up before it really got started because we would eventually have to go long distance. He convinced me otherwise.

Brandon is a great man. He brought me flowers, helped me celebrate my half birthday, and made me laugh a lot. As time went on, we bonded more, spent more time together, and I began to want to hold hands and cuddle and, dare I say, *kiss.*

These were things I had never done before. I didn't know how long one had to wait. What's the right timing for everything? Who decides—me or him? All I knew is that it was time. He was my boyfriend. I wanted to lay one on him. But it was my first-ever kiss and he knew that.

It was not his first kiss. I have yet to know the pressure of introducing someone to kissing. Because of my age, I doubt that will be a burden I'll have to bear, but again, you never know. So, one week after school ended and about a month before we were to start our long-distance relationship, Brandon invited me out to dinner and a movie. A classic date night, and he told me there was a surprise afterward.

As we drove toward the mountains later that night, he asked, "Bridget, do you have any guesses as to where we're going?"

"McDonald's for ice cream?" I knew we weren't going to McDonald's.

"No."

"Oh really? I was really hoping we were. I'll be disappointed in anything else." I was nervous. I'm sure he was too. "Are we going to outer space? I'd like that, I've never been there."

"Close."

We drove up the mountainside to a spot that overlooked Tucson, our beloved desert city. Brandon wanted to make the experience perfect for me and memorable. I was honored and wanted that too.

Being the romantic that I am, I had built up this idea in my head of what my first kiss would feel like. I mean, so many of the romantic comedies I grew up with probably didn't help.

The Princess Diaries had us believing in the fabled "foot pop" when you have your first kiss with someone. Pop culture has us believing these moments feel like fireworks.

There we were, cuddled up together in a blanket, looking at the stars over our town, our faces nice and close, and eventually he bravely laid one on me. Our lips met, and although it was my first-ever kiss, it felt familiar. There were no fireworks or foot pops. It was just a nice moment. A rite of passage. It was the next step in our relationship, and it made perfect sense. There was nothing awkward about it. Nothing weird. It was sweet and good.

It hadn't occurred to me that it didn't live up to the mind-blowing experience I had come to expect until Brandon went back to his car to grab another blanket because it was getting colder. I stood there on the side of the mountain, looking down at the orange-lit city and then up again at the expanse of stars that I didn't normally see from day to day. It was breathtaking.

And that's when God whispered. *So . . . what do you think?*

"About the kiss? I mean, it was fine. Not what I expected, but that's better than it being bad."

What about all this? God asked, referring to the scene that lay before me.

"It's gorgeous."

Breathtaking, if you will, he whispered.

"I will," I said.

See, Brandon really got something right that night by bringing me to the mountains for my first kiss. He knew we needed to pair the big moment with a special place, some good scenery, and a little romance. What he didn't know is that God would steal the show. I can give no credit to my only-ever boyfriend/first kiss for taking my breath away that night. He hadn't. No offense to him—he's a wonderful guy.

God met me with the realest truth that night. This would be the first of many times he would meet me on mountainsides to let me know that life is all about him and how romantic that really is. Even the greatest love stories of all time pale in comparison to the reality of our story with Jesus.

ROMANCE IS FOR EVERYONE

Unfortunately, my middle school file of letters to my husband was lost to a computer crash, so I waited until I had my own laptop to pick the habit back up. I think I wrote those letters because I didn't want to forget who I was before marriage. I didn't want my future husband to think that my life started with him. It hadn't. My life started on October 26, 1989. And long before that, really.

Sometimes, we can get caught up thinking our lives don't begin until we finally have the thing we always wanted—a relationship, sex, marriage, kids, a career. And then we find out we were living all along and none of those things answered the ache in our souls for more. How do we answer that desire for romance as single people? Do we have to wait for another person till we experience it? I don't think so.

God has convinced me that he is the most romantic one. If there's ever a contest, he wins.

First of all, he went *way* out of his way, showed up knocking at our doors (he uses this image in Revelation 3:20), and died to have us. His love knew no bounds—discomfort, humanity, suffering, death. He conquered it all for our love.

A few years ago, I was ordered by my supervisors to take a retreat of silence in the desert. They knew this place just outside of Tucson in the Saguaro National Park called the Desert House of Prayer, where total silence is observed among visitors as a holy act of trust and listening.

I had an equal amount of desire and dread going into my thirty-six hours of silence. I am a very chatty lady. Asked a simple question, I will often respond with a thirty-minute story instead of a simple yes or no. The people who love this quality of mine have stuck around, while others walk away probably thinking I should just write a book already. Joke's on them.

Going into this retreat of silence, I was not sure what would come of it. I knew my supervisor wanted me to experience God's voice outside of my normal context, but I didn't know what I should be looking forward to. At the time, I was incredibly stressed out. My anxiety and stress were leading to weird health issues I had never struggled with before. During this season my students often said, "Bridget, you're always sick!" When it got to that point, I knew something was very wrong.

I just hoped that thirty-six silent hours in the desert would solve all my problems. Have you ever been there? Thinking that one weekend, one spiritual experience will make all the yuck go away?

Well, God is more merciful than that. What I'm learning about him is that he is gracious to slowly reveal how we have been impacted by our life experiences—choosing the most optimal moments when he knows we will listen.

So, there I was at the end of a warm February, with nothing to do but wait for my big moment with God in which he would tidy up the mess of my lonely heart. For the first couple hours, nothing really happened. I got settled in, lay on my bed in

silence, and wandered around the premises, exploring the resources they offered. When I found a selection of incredibly
cool handmade walking sticks, I decided to go on a solo hike
into the cactus-covered hills.

Hiking through the desert can be both beautiful and very
uncomfortable. There's little shade and prickly plants at every
turn. Not to mention the chance of coming across any number
of terrifying or harmless desert critters in their natural
habitat. I set out mildly nervous because I had only ever hiked
with friends and was usually the slowest one in the group.

I love nature. I love being outside—I spent as much of my
childhood outside as possible. I am attracted to outdoorsy
guys. But am I outdoorsy? I don't know. I'm not indoorsy.
Maybe I'm just backyardsy. Patiosy. Leisurely strollsy.

Either way, I was glad to set my own pace and see a new part
of the Sonoran Desert that I had so come to love. Below the
clear blue sky, as the breeze gently brushed my face, I wondered what God would tell me. Eventually, the trail led to a
delightful canyon, which I imagined once had water rushing
through it, and I found an awkward yet shady place to sit and
pull out my Bible.

I paused a moment to listen for what I should read, anticipating a Scripture that would tie the solution to my problems
up in a neat little bow.

Read Song of Songs.

"What? . . . No."

. . . Nothing.

"God, look. Song of Songs isn't for me. I'm single. I'm
somewhat virginal. What's the point of me reading that book?"

Are only parts of the Bible for you, Bridget? Or the whole thing?

I sighed. "The whole thing . . ."

And what is the whole thing about?

"Us."

Read Song of Songs.

So, I did. I read it three times that weekend, and it blew my mind.

In Song of Songs, the bride longs for her husband, and he delights in her at every turn. She searches for him and is satisfied in him. He loves everything good about her.

In the soft breeze of the desert place, my God whispered to me that I am his bride, and he is my bridegroom. He delights in every part of me. He wants me to search for him and find him, to long for him and delight in him.

But could I believe that he finds me as beautiful and perfect as the husband in Song of Songs finds his bride? Could I see his romance at every turn, wooing me, showing me my worth and his many thoughts of me?

That was God's sole invitation to me that weekend. He did not fix all my problems, but he beckoned me closer to him, into deeper intimacy. He wanted me to see myself the way he sees me, as beloved, precious, and beautiful.

A LOVE STRONGER THAN DEATH

I'm afraid we've had it so wrong. We have forgotten our most intimate lover. The one who created our bodies, sex, and desire itself! The one who intended that we would be close with him first and foremost. He is not far from the spaces where we long to be seen, understood, loved, known, and delighted in. He created them.

He is the Most Romantic One. He wants us to see that this romance is for everyone—in and out of romantic human relationships. Romance is for the everyday. It's a gift from God to make the mundane come to life and the bleak things of this world come to light.

> Place me like a seal over your heart,
> like a seal on your arm;

> for love is as strong as death,
> its jealousy unyielding as the grave.

> It burns like blazing fire,
> like a mighty flame.

> Many waters cannot quench love;
> rivers cannot sweep it away.

> If one were to give
> all the wealth of one's house for love,
> it would be utterly scorned.

(Song of Songs 8:6-7)

Even the bride longed to be sealed on the heart of her groom. She knew the power of love, that their earthly love was only a shadow of the Lord's flame for us. His undeniable, unquenchable, unending, incomparable love for us is worth more than all the wealth of our lives. God's love looks like many, many things—but as depicted in Song of Songs, it's fiercely romantic.

Are you convinced yet? Don't worry, I'm praying this over us: "Lord, we believe, help our unbelief" (see Mark 9:24).

The most romantic story of all is that of a God who left his holy place to come and save us, his loves, from certain death.

Think of all the love stories we hear growing up—all the same elements are there: praise and adoration, longing, sacrifice, salvation from suffering, and usually a happy ending. When I was younger, I was most compelled by love stories when one person would declare they could not live without the other. I had this deep ache in my soul that told me that someday, someone would come along who would rather die than live without me. Luckily, I have matured enough to know that's a really unreasonable expectation to have, not to mention a bit egocentric. But I could never shake that ache in my soul to be chosen and loved to death.

I don't think I ever will be able to shake this desire to be romanced beyond reason. I need a love that is bigger than life. The Song of Songs bride and I have something in common. A desire for love that's stronger than death. A love willing to risk it all.

God loved us from the start. He created us even though he knew we would turn on him. He knew that many of us would look to solve this deep ache in ways other than unity with him. He delights in us on every level; he knows who we are, he knows what he made. He longs for us and has given us freedom to love him in return. And even though the cost was high—leaving his throne and touching dirt and sickness and being rejected by us—we were worth it to him. He makes it very clear that even just one of us would be worth it to him (Matthew 18:12).

Jesus came to give us resurrection life—life that comes after death. Nothing else like this is available to us. You can't get eternal life and steadfast love from a human relationship.

I have longed for romantic love for a long time, but it's always been in my reach. I have never been far from my dreams realized. How beautiful is that? Jesus embodies my soul's deepest longing. He is the Most Romantic One. The story of Jesus' death and resurrection is just one of the ways Creator God has shown us his divine romance!

Pilgrimage Moment: Practicing Presence

"The heavens declare the glory of God; the skies proclaim the work of his hands" (Psalm 19:1).

When I talk about romance, I'm really talking about practicing presence. This means slowing down to notice the countless ways that God displays his glory, which is most beautiful to behold. There are so many wonderful things that God has given to us freely, besides eternal salvation and relationship with him.

Imagine with me some of the ways God demonstrates romance to us. Let's do a little exercise with the five senses. If you don't have all five senses, use the ones you do have! I recommend going outside for this one, but if that's not available to you, just take a couple minutes in your location to become present. I will name a sense, ask a question, and then share some of the best sensations I've experienced. If it's easier for you to become present after reading through mine, feel free to do so.

TOUCH: What is something you can feel right now?
There are times when the weather is perfect, the air against my skin makes me buzz with excitement, and I can tangibly *feel* eternity. It might be the temperature of heaven, but there's something about it that my soul knows well. It makes me feel invincible.

SIGHT: What are a few things you can see right now that inspire you?
I've never felt more in love, more in awe, my breath more taken, my joy more heightened, than in nature. Think about stars, for example! Humans are so smitten by astronomy. I could stand out in the open, the vast expanse of a night sky above me, the fuzzy Milky Way showing off, my mouth agape, for hours. Every day when the sun fully sets here in the desert, I swoon over the way the mountains are silhouetted against the darkening sky. I get saved all over again in nature.

TASTE: What is the taste on your tongue right now? Or why don't you go have a snack?

There's a scene in the movie *Ratatouille* in which Remy the rat is tasting cheese and grapes and little fireworks are simultaneously going off in his mind and mouth. That's how I feel when I eat goat cheese. Or *elote*. I know God exists because he made the people who make *elote*—a mouthwatering mayonnaise and crumbly cheese–covered corn on the cob drizzled in lime juice and tajín. I feel the divine in every bite. When I traveled to China, the unending combinations of delicious things they do with vegetables brought me to my knees in praise. Real Chinese food is proof of God's great love for us. There's nothing like delicious nourishment to help me feel cradled in the Lord's arms.

SMELL: What is a smell or two you can detect in the air right now?

When you walk into a sub sandwich shop that first smell of bread hits deep. The scent of fresh roses lights up my whole being. Or consider the wild phenomenon when you're minding your business and you are transported just by a whiff of something and memories come flooding in from a different time, a different place. How is that not the most magical experience? It's basically teleportation.

HEARING: What can you hear right now?

Some songs can lift you up, bring out your emotions, wake up things in you that you haven't felt in a while. I love being in a sea of people at a concert, soaking in all the sounds, feeling the vibrations, and yet having this beautiful experience of solitude in the midst of it all. That quiet place inside of sound is so romantic to me. It's one of my favorite experiences.

You can see, taste, feel, smell, and hear God's romance for us every day. His is all the good stuff of life. And it's ours for the taking, so we shouldn't miss it! It's so important to practice this. To understand that romance is innate to how God set this whole thing up. It was meant to be breathtakingly beautiful in every way. We were meant to feel the heights and depths of love every hour.

If you haven't slowed down to practice presence yet, here's a great guideline for when you do:

Go on a walk in your neighborhood if you can, or go sit outside.

First, take some deep breaths and center yourself in your body.

Start with sight—what are five things you notice when you look around?

Then sound—what are four things you can hear when you really listen?

And touch—what are three things you feel in your body or outside of it?

Then smell—what are two smells you sense in the air around you?

Lastly, taste—what taste lingers in your mouth from today?

This practice will surely help you become more present to being alive, and it may foster gratefulness, inspiration, and divine romance in you.

MADE FOR THIS

Romance is often reduced to one context, sometimes because it's confused with what's been taught about sex in the evangelical church. The traditional biblical sexual ethic includes a covenantal relationship between a man and a woman, and instructs that this be the only person you engage with sexually.

Now, whether that is *your* sexual ethic or practice, I think you have probably been shaped by it one way or another. You may still carry the belief that the good stuff can only happen in the context of marriage or your relationship with your "soulmate." I do believe that a covenant relationship is the best context for sex, but I believe there's a lot of other things that don't have to be reserved for marriage.

Like being deeply loved and being celebrated.

Being sensual.

Being protected, taken care of, and delighted in.

Feeling delight.

Having a best friend.

Having life-changing conversations.

Robert Farrar Capon was an Episcopal priest; I share a birthday with him. Our lives overlapped by fewer than twenty-four years, and I didn't know he existed until long after he was gone. I don't believe in soulmates, but I do believe that God makes some of us so alike that intangible qualities connect us.

When I first read his book *The Supper of the Lamb*, I was enamored by the poetic and holy ways Capon saw the world—food, delight, the process of cooking. It's like he had words for sentiments only my heart understood. Capon was a fellow romantic. He offered himself fully in his books; he was funny, clever, prophetic, and wise. I never knew the man, but he is definitely a priest and friend of mine. Here's what he has to say about romance:

> You indict me, no doubt, as an incurable romantic. I plead guilty without contest. I see no other explanation of what we are about. Why do we marry, why take friends and lovers, why give ourselves to music, painting, chemistry, or cooking? Out of simple delight in the resident goodness of creation, of course; but out of more than that, too. Half of earth's gorgeousness lies hidden in the glimpsed city it longs to become. For all its rooted loveliness, the world has no continuing city here; it is an outlandish place, a foreign home, a session in via to a better

version of itself—and it is our glory to see it so and thirst
until Jerusalem comes home at last. We were given ap-
petites, not to consume the world and forget it, but to
taste its goodness and hunger to make it great.[1]

Doesn't he capture that beautifully? He accomplishes many
things in this quote. First of all, he openly accepts his romantic
nature. And then he offers a grace that we don't offer ourselves
often enough—we are made this way! We are meant to delight.
Secondly, he pivots to a deeper spiritual truth—we are still
longing for a greater reality. Our romanticism points to a reality that we were made for the greater future in which everything is made new and everything is whole (Revelation 21). In
one short paragraph, he helps me see that my longing is
natural and proof of the Divine.

We were made to be lovers and friends and have hobbies
and nerd out about the good stuff in life. But rather than leave
it at that, we get to practice slowing down and recognizing
that the things we long for are mere shadows of what is to
come. The best of the best things are still only glimpses
of heaven.

Sometimes, when I get lost in my thoughts of romantic
things, I start to realize how it's God's grace that he even lets
us see his beauty and majesty, and experience his deli-
ciousness. He did not have to give us so many happy reasons
to be alive. He did not have to make us easily inspired people
who coo our oohs and ahs at lights and fireworks. He did not
have to make taste buds! He did not have to make babies,
puppies, and kittens. But wow, isn't he romantic and creative,
and just so kind?

Seeing God this way might not connect with you at all. You
might not consider yourself very romantic, but I'm not

convinced. Consider why your walls go up when thinking about God as the most intimate love of our lives. It could be how you were taught. You could be oversexualizing romance. Or perhaps you are more a thinker than a feeler. But anywhere there's delight, there's romance. Slow down a little to get out of your head and into your body and the room you're in. Savor your favorite meal. Put on some music you like and just listen. Light a scented candle. Draw a warm bath. Climb on your roof and watch the sunset. Enjoy.

Romance is about enjoyment. And God has given us so much to enjoy. All the things I mentioned above were outside the context of a romantic relationship. Experiencing romance means practicing presence, being available to what's in front of you. Someday, that might be a special person. Being present and available to others is vital to healthy relationships. If you can revel in the divine of your friends, family members, and partners, you will also have grace and love for them in the moments when it's hard.

To me, romance is a direct combatant to the apathy and hatred in our world. It's a salve for negativity and deceit. When things suck, it's important to take a step back and take stock of what doesn't. Weigh the good against all the bad, not to erase the bad or hide from it, but to have perspective.

Without romantic eyes, we cannot see all that. Without eyes to see mystery, intrigue, and excitement, we will drown in a pit of big bad darkness. So maybe you need to turn on your romantic eyes. Let God alight the part of you that can see, taste, hear, feel, and smell the divinity all around you. You don't have to wait until you are in a romantic relationship to experience that.

LOVE THAT LASTS FOREVER

Brandon and I broke up two days before I left for a trip to Rome. I found myself on a tour bus in the land of pasta and gelato with no appetite and a broken heart. I could barely pay attention to the audio tour in my headset that described the ancient sites out the window.

"God, I just don't get it," I prayed in my head. "How can I be so *un*chosen? What does it take to be forever loved?" This was not the first time and wouldn't be the last time I asked such questions of God.

Listen.

I refocused on the audio tour and the world outside my window. We passed a large stone timeline of the rise and fall of the ancient Roman Empire. The recording claimed that Rome was one of the greatest empires in history.

Look at the timeline, when I was here, God whispered to my soul again.

I looked, and there in the beginnings of the Common Era was the height of the greatest empire to have ever ruled the earth. Not long after Jesus' life, death, and resurrection, and after Peter was crucified in that very city, Rome fell.

And where are you now, Bridget? You are a tourist in the ruins and rubble of the world's greatest known kingdom. But my kingdom? It reigns forevermore (Daniel 6:26). *My love for you is an everlasting love* (Jeremiah 31:3). *When I came for you, it was to choose you and give you a life in a kingdom that never ends* (1 Peter 2:9). *A love that is stronger than death, a reality that will never crumble and fall, like Rome eventually did.*

That was the most romantic moment of my life so far. God opened my ears and eyes to see his great romance for me in the midst of my heartache. He spoke truth to me and a future for me that was full of hope. And that has been true so far. The rest of this book is proof of his steadfast love in my all my life's highs and lows. In all the years to come, I would remain single and still experience the greatest love of my life.

3

COMMUNITY PART ONE: WHEN YOU HAVE IT

I'm a little embarrassed to admit that my whole life, I've been chasing friendships with an energy unmatched by those around me. When I was especially busy in high school, my dad used to say, "Your friends are your hobby." Any free time I had, I was with my friends. And I had *so many* friends. Probably too many, which might have been what my dad was getting at. But I couldn't get enough of them.

I had something right about the desire to be surrounded by friends. Friendships might be the single most important type of relationship you can have. In its purest and most natural form, friendship is truly a "just because" in your life, based on an ineffable connection that makes a certain person stick around. Famous single theologian and writer Henri Nouwen says it best:

> Friendship is one of the greatest gifts a human being can receive. It is a bond beyond common goals, common interests, or common histories. It is a bond stronger than sexual union can create, deeper than a shared fate can solidify, and even more intimate than the bonds of marriage or community. Friendship is being with the other

in joy and sorrow, even when we cannot increase the joy or decrease the sorrow. It is a unity of souls that gives nobility and sincerity to love. Friendship makes all of life shine brightly. Blessed are those who lay down their lives for their friends.[1]

That is what I spent so much of my time chasing. Sometimes I had the best of it, and sometimes I was left wanting. Entering adulthood, though, I'm not sure I knew to expect the type of friendship and community coming my way.

My first year out of college was a dream—just ask any of the Laughterns, my InterVarsity intern team with whom I lived for a year in Boulder, Colorado. There were five of us: my roommates, Ivanna and Kathryn, and the guys next door, Tom and Daniel. From the start, we all agreed to a certain level of commitment and intentionality with one another during our year of leading college ministry together. We decided to live in the same apartment complex right off campus and set aside time just to be with each other. What followed was one of the most rewarding years of my life.

Romance was *not* my concern that year. In fact, I think we were all under the impression that if we started our internship year single, we should probably remain that way for most of it so we could invest our time and energy in community and personal growth. Sometimes you need seasons like this when lack of romance is a nonissue. To be honest, with four best friends always around, I didn't feel I was lacking anything relationally.

Sunday nights were intern nights: no work, only fun. After too many weird movie nights, we made an activity jar and went out and did fun things around town. We visited breweries, picked outfits for each other at Ross Dress for Less, bought each other random gifts at Target, played truth or dare. We cooked and laughed and played board games. We argued about the end of *Inception* and spent a good thirty minutes pretending to be suspended in the van flying off the bridge like at the end of the movie. We had deep conversations and worked through conflict together. I'll never forget all the times I came home from campus after a hard meeting with a student and had a friend there to talk to and pray with, or all the late nights sitting on the kitchen floor whispering funny stories about our part-time gigs.

That first year after college shaped my view of what community can be. Real community is vital to having a vibrant experience in your singleness. We all long to be a part of something, to be loved and known, to be heard and understood. Consider the first days of the Christ-following community:

> They devoted themselves to the apostles' teaching and to fellowship, to the breaking of bread and to prayer. Everyone was filled with awe at the many wonders and signs performed by the apostles. All the believers were together and had everything in common. They sold property and possessions to give to anyone who had need. Every day they continued to meet together in the temple courts. They broke bread in their homes and ate together with glad and sincere hearts, praising God and enjoying the favor of all the people. And the Lord added to their number daily those who were being saved. (Acts 2:42-47)

We the Laughterns were in a beautiful bubble like the one described in Acts. We were there with the students, devoting ourselves to the teachings of the apostles, inviting others in, eating, laughing, and praying together. We engaged with each other's issues, learned together, had fun together, and addressed conflict as it came up. We learned to be vulnerable and trust each other. We shared our time, hearts, and resources with one another. God did amazing things among us that year and some of our friends became followers of Jesus. It was the best experience of community I've had yet.

More than a decade later, I can confidently say that this type of community is rare. I think that's why Luke described it with detail in Acts. It was wild that people of all different backgrounds came together like a family, with commitment and love for one another, even when conflict arose. It was a true sign of the Holy Spirit at work, and I believe he was at work in us too.

SECURITY, SIGHT, AND SPACE

Healthy, life-giving community is an ideal context for spiritual growth and healing. Why? Because security goes a long way. In his book *The Soul of Desire*, Curt Thompson says, "Security is about being able, in the face of feeling seen, soothed, and safe, to move away from our relational base and step out to take the risk of new adventure."[2] For the first time in my adult life, I had the most concentrated experience of feeling "seen, soothed, and safe" by my intern team.

There's security in being loved intentionally and unconditionally. My teammates didn't have unrealistic expectations of me; they believed in who I was and who I could be. They delighted in me and took me seriously every day. They let me ugly cry when things were hard, and they trusted me to hold their stories as well. We were safe to work through conflict together and felt secure in coming home to one another.

Because I felt so secure in my community, I began to see myself more clearly. I started to recognize old patterns and broken perspectives I had been carrying since childhood. Eventually that sight gave way to making more space for spiritual growth and healing.

One opportunity that helped me see myself during my internship year was life coaching. I had only heard about life coaching on *Oprah*, and it seemed goofy at the time, but all my teammates were considering it, and they encouraged me to go to the thirty-minute one-on-one session with Coach Jenny. So, I did. I entered feeling skeptical, which is unusual for me. But it was one of the first times I felt really exposed. I knew that she could see me, and I didn't like what we were seeing.

In thirty minutes, Jenny pointed out that I don't seem to receive love very well—I don't naturally trust people to love me. At first, I was super annoyed because *Wow, that is not me, what are you talking about?* But I walked away knowing that she was right. She encouraged me to do the work of looking at my family relationships and how those issues might have originated, which I had never really done before. I planned to meet with her for twelve weeks during the spring semester.

The reason I was unable to see myself clearly was because I had spent so much of my time and energy on the people around me. I made my world about my people. I was very good at being a good friend, a good daughter, a good student, a good leader. I knew how to earn praise, affirmation, and affection. Perhaps when my dad noted that my friends were my hobby, he was commenting on something much deeper: I spent an inordinate amount of time on everyone else.

Life coaching was a great way to make space and look at what was really going on inside of me. I entered the twelve weeks with Jenny with an itch to fix a pattern in my relationships. I would get close to a guy friend—right up to the point of dating—and then . . . nothing. The guy didn't seem to want to date me. It was heartbreaking and confusing. I didn't want it to happen again. And I wanted to know what was wrong with me. In every other type of relationship, I seemed to know how to win love and affection, but with men, I couldn't get there. I was always a best friend and never a girlfriend.

But Jenny is a great coach. She didn't come in trying to fix my dating life. She wanted to see me have some freedom in my patterns. She wanted to help me uncover hidden truths about myself. She helped me recognize this voice inside my head that kept telling me not to trust people's love for me and to keep trying to earn it.

As I expressed my desire to be better and do better because I was now a campus minister and I had to set an example, Jenny heard and saw something that I never would have: it wasn't just love that I didn't receive well, it was grace.

The irony of it all is that I am an evangelist before anything else. I believe that the good news of Jesus' life, death, and resurrection is for everyone and that it's freely given, undeserved. I want everyone to know that story and be transformed by it. But for some reason, my favorite story of all, one that had captured my heart for decades, hadn't totally sunk in for me.

I was crushed by this realization.

My knee-jerk reaction was to fix it and prescribe myself some regular devotional time every morning, as a supplement to my hypocrisy and shame. How could I not believe the gospel for myself? How could I believe it and yet not fully receive it as my own? I think this was such a blow to me because I've made my entire life about Jesus—there's nothing I'm more convinced about, excited about, happy to be a part of, and year by year, this becomes truer! I felt like a hypocrite.

Gently and tenderly, and with so much grace and love, Jenny helped me see what was really going on for me. This was the beginning of me noticing God's great mercy on my life. In his great love for us, he does not leave unaddressed the things that bind us.

Behind all that shame was a confession: I had been struggling with masturbation and pornography for a couple years. I didn't want to bring that into ministry with me. It didn't have an addictive hold on me, I was just ashamed it was a part of my story at all. I had already confessed to many of my close friends for accountability and encouragement, but I was sad to admit that it hadn't completely fizzled away.

When I told Jenny, as when I had told so many others before, the world didn't end. I wasn't punished or fired or shamed. Instead, she opened a whole world of new thought for me. Jenny compared our human brokenness to an octopus—it's one creature with many different arms attached to us. The work we were about to do was to peel off just one of the tentacles. (This Octopus of Brokenness has become a bit of a character in my life, visiting another tentacle with each passing season.)

Rather than create a list of spiritual disciplines for me to check off week by week, we were going to gently and curiously ask how I landed there. Why was I turning to sexual gratification? Why was I having a hard time with grace? Why didn't I trust others to love me well?

First, Jenny invited me to start considering my own sexual ethic. She told me that some Christians don't think masturbation is unbiblical and that I should decide for myself. I had never considered that as an option. I hadn't felt like conversations about sex and sexuality in Christian community were productive. But I wasn't ready for the idea of a healthy sexual ethic as a single person that included self-pleasure. What I knew at the time was that for me, all the thoughts and motivations surrounding my own self-gratification were messy. I turned to masturbation and pornography because of unmet longings. I longed to be loved, but I felt so unloved and unchosen. I was unwilling to admit that. I would rather have admitted that something was wrong with me, something making me unlovable and unworthy, than to admit that I just wanted to be loved.

To admit that you want to be loved feels weak. To be a Christian and confess that you feel a major deficit in love and affection in your life feels wrong. Unholy, almost. The Christian culture I grew up in told me to snuff out anything having to do with desire. Flesh becomes the enemy. Body becomes a curse. But this isn't true to the gospel, thank God!

Our bodies are a gift. Our longings are natural. My desire to be loved was normal. The problem was that I had a block. I didn't think I deserved any of the love that was coming my way. I was in an endless feedback loop of unworthiness and shame over and over again.

I did a really good job of keeping busy to ignore it. More friends. More social life. More ministry. More service. But the heartache persisted. Shame over my heartache continued. And so, I coped by taking matters into my own hands quite literally. You can see why I found myself in this recurring loop—unwilling to address unmet needs in healthy ways, coping with unhealthy self-gratification, and then feeling ashamed of my choices and unworthy of love all over again. I was seriously in need of some freedom.

Jenny offered a new approach to my unmet longings. She asked why, when I'm tempted to cope this way, are my only options to either *sin* or *not sin*? What if instead, my options were to either *sin* or *honor my longings*? Any number of things could honor my longings: creating or producing something new and beautiful, exercising and using my body in satisfying ways, cooking something delicious, delighting in creation. So many more ways to honor our longings come to mind when we slow down to think about it.

Unmet longings can lead us down the path to habitual sin. We take the easy route and the cheap option as quick fixes. But God has given us so many ways to say yes to our longings and to honor what's going on inside us. Masturbation when paired with porn is a distraction and coping mechanism that can often have harmful implications.

This was just the beginning of figuring out my own story. For so long I didn't think I had a substantial testimony, that my sin was just internal, run-of-the-mill stuff. But the older I got, the more I saw myself and my life for what it was—desperately in need of Jesus. Life with him looked wildly different than I had originally thought.

What if life with Jesus was more beautiful, free, and alive than I ever knew? There I was inviting others to say yes to a life I wasn't sure I fully knew yet. Much of my life coaching centered around stepping into this real life with Jesus. It was beautiful and messy and hard because unlearning old beliefs and stepping out of old patterns takes time.

As I grappled with these deep issues, my roommates were there to pray for me and let me cry, and they listened while I shared what I was learning. They loved me just the same. Sometimes they totally related. Things that felt taboo or scary to talk about no longer were. Being in community with them helped prove wrong all my insecurities and fears. I was loved just because. I did nothing to earn it. The reality of their love and grace freely given made it easy to envision a version of myself who could be free from my old beliefs and patterns. Grace and love could be mine. I started to offer myself a grace I never had before.

All of this was making me a better campus minister. If I was able to receive the fullness of Jesus' grace, then what I was extending to my students would look, feel, and taste more like the kingdom of God. When you begin to address the root of your problems, it makes it easier to live in grace. It makes deeper and more loving friendships and relationships.

What I had originally thought was simply weird guy/girl dating dynamics and sexual sin was much deeper. I needed to accept that nothing I did could earn the love of the Father—nothing I did outside of believing in the gospel would save me. Even to the very last meeting with Jenny in early May, I still communicated my desire to prove myself, my residual unwillingness to receive the grace Jesus had for me.

Many of us chase other things because we believe that through them we can secure our value, worth, and salvation. And that's our big lie, isn't it?

A PILGRIMAGE BACK IN TIME

During our last meeting, Jenny invited me to do inner healing prayer, which is a form of prayer that requires a lot of listening, faith, and holy imagination. Consequently, I was a bit skeptical about it . . . when did I become such a skeptic? I had grown up in the charismatic church, for crying out loud! Ultimately, I was willing to try. Jenny explained to me that before we started, we were going to create a scenario in which I felt safe, so that as we dove into my memories, I could return to that place if I needed. I imagined myself on this tiny dock on a lake behind my aunt's house. It was always serene there.

Then we prayed for a core memory that might be the root of my unwillingness to receive grace. Even though I was skeptical, I couldn't get this one memory out of my head. It was an anecdote I would tell when describing how funny growing up Pentecostal could be.

When I was about seven years old, my dad picked me up from children's church on a Wednesday night and led me back into the sanctuary after the service. There was an older woman I didn't know waiting there, and my dad had her pray over me. I understood that he was hoping I would be "baptized in the Holy Spirit." The woman cradled me in her arms and started praying while rocking me back and forth. I didn't like it because I didn't know her, but I trusted my dad and I trusted God.

In my head I told God, "I don't want to get slain in the Spirit like I've seen so many grownups do." It looked scary, and as a child you have very little control in your life—only over your movement and your mouth, and even that is policed to some degree. While in this lady's arms, I also remember asking God, "What did I do wrong? Why are we doing this?" God didn't answer those questions for me that night, but he did answer my prayer. Nothing Pentecostal happened to my little body or tongue. I was still Bridget, who loved Jesus more than anything else.

Going through the McDonald's drive thru on the way home, I asked, "Dad, why did you do that? Why did you have that lady pray for me?" It's amazing to think about the wild things we will put up with as children under the logic of our parents.

I remember my dad saying, "Well, honey, a part of following Jesus is being filled with the Holy Spirit, and I want you to be baptized in the Holy Spirit so that you may be close to God. One way that we know this has happened is when people speak in tongues. You should pray that God would baptize you in his Holy Spirit."

Made enough sense to me. The problem is that children are poor interpreters of life. Every night from ages seven to fourteen, I would look up at the night sky from my bedroom window and ask God to fill me with the Holy Spirit. I asked him to make it obvious. I wanted to be a good Christian and a good daughter. I was under the impression that this was the last big thing I was missing as a follower of Jesus. But I never communicated those things to my dad.

As I described this story to Jenny, I began to see the gravity of that memory. It told it as a funny anecdote because it left a mark on me. It was definitely a turning point in my relationship with God. Not that there's anything wrong with a child praying for the Holy Spirit, but the theology instilled in me that night was not of the Spirit of God.

For some of my most formative years, I believed that I had to earn my salvation and prove it. I believed that I wasn't fully saved or whole.

Jenny helped me reimagine that memory. She had twenty-three-year-old me tell seven-year-old me the truth. She had seven-year-old and twenty-three-year-old me tell God and my dad how we felt. I told my younger self that she had done nothing wrong. I told God that the experience wasn't funny, but actually made me really sad. The impact it had on me was lasting. In the memory, I told my dad I didn't like that he did that and that I thought his theology was wrong. It felt good to take that memory seriously and reclaim it for what it was.

After we reimagined the memory, I returned to the dock. Jenny asked me to imagine Jesus there. And we asked Jesus, "What do you say after all of this?"

I sensed Jesus saying, *All I have is yours. I would lasso the sun out of the sky for you, Bridget.*

Jenny prayed a blessing that Jesus did grab the sun from the sky and give it to me to as a gift to fill me up with his light. Then she asked, "How do you feel? What is your and Jesus' response to that?"

I pictured Jesus inviting me to jump into the water to swim and play. He wanted to celebrate this new freedom. I realized that fifteen years before, an attempt at a sort of baptism was made on my life (before my actual water baptism even happened). And here at twenty-three, Jesus and I got in the water together, to enter this new life in which I would receive his grace and be filled! I could be his child again, not responsible for my own salvation.

I was beginning to feel true freedom.

I called my dad later that day and asked him if he remembered doing that when I was seven. He said he didn't, but he believed me when I said it happened. I was surprised by his response: as a taste of God's grace for me so early in this new life, my dad apologized. He could see how weird and uncomfortable that would have been, and he understood how my childlike interpretation of those events messed me up! It was balm to my soul to hear my dad understand and believe me.

I'm choosing to call this activity that Jenny had me do a "pilgrimage back in time" because we bravely went on a journey back in my memories to learn something new about me in order to help me move forward in my present reality. There are many versions of this kind of pilgrimage, not just inner healing prayer. You can do some narrative journaling about your life. Describe things in as much detail as you can muster, and take time to ask God where he was in the midst of it all. You can call your parents or childhood friends and ask them to share with you their impressions of your upbringing and who you were, for better or worse. Sometimes, in order to move forward, you have to consider your past.

For me, this pilgrimage back in time was done in a safe context with a professional. I highly recommend the same for you when you endeavor to travel back in time. We must be gentle with our pasts. The experience of remembering trauma can trigger unexpected responses, so it's worth the time and investment to do this with a therapist. If therapy and life coaching would stretch you financially, take some time to look for more affordable programs—they exist. I have taken advantage of many of them.

WHEN YOUR FRIENDS ARE ALL DATING, AND YOU'RE STILL SINGLE

Six weeks after life coaching ended, we were all at Inter-Varsity's orientation for new staff. So much had shifted. I was about to move back to Arizona for full-time ministry at Northern Arizona University; all of my teammates were in re-lationships, and I was the only one who was single, Even though so much excitement was on the horizon for us, I was super sad about leaving the Laughterns. They had come to be a family for me.

I was starting to panic. The closer we got to going our sep-arate ways, the more I worried. Would I ever have such a special experience like this again? Would I ever feel more loved, connected, supported, and safe? My teammates all had someone to hold on to, but I was about to float off into the Great Unknown without the security of our intern team. Honestly, I don't think it was a terrible fear to have. When you have something that special, it's shocking and sad to leave it, especially when you think you're the only one feeling the loss.

It can be hard when all your friends are in relationships and you're not. This has been increasingly common in my adult life. It's normal. It's natural for people to find love, get married, start families. But it's still difficult to lose the attention and time with your friends when they are investing in their new relationships. Nothing really prepares you for it.

I didn't share my feelings with my team, but my roommate at orientation encouraged me to get prayer ministry, so I signed up for a time slot. The way we do prayer ministry in InterVarsity is similar to the inner healing prayer Jenny did with me six weeks prior. I went to my appointment and met with a campus minister named Kaylyn. We had never met before that week, but I shared my feelings with her openly. We started our prayer time by listening together, and the story of Jesus visiting Mary and Martha's house came up.

> As Jesus and his disciples were on their way, he came to a village where a woman named Martha opened her home to him. She had a sister called Mary, who sat at the Lord's feet listening to what he said. But Martha was distracted by all the preparations that had to be made. She came to him and asked, "Lord, don't you care that my sister has left me to do the work by myself? Tell her to help me!"
>
> "Martha, Martha," the Lord answered, "you are worried and upset about many things, but few things are needed— or indeed only one. Mary has chosen what is better, and it will not be taken away from her." (Luke 10:38-42)

"Which of these women do you most relate to, Bridget?" Kaylyn asked me.

Too often I found myself like Martha, rushing around trying to prove my worth, value, and even holiness. As I felt my community slipping through my fingers, I could feel the temptation rise in me to continue in these same patterns: to cling to the love and affection I have, to make sure it doesn't go anywhere. I may have even felt a little abandoned by my team, as though I was left to do all this work of community alone. I shared that with Kaylyn. She prayed a blessing of Mary over me.

Jesus' invitation for me in this transitional period was to sit at his feet and enjoy his presence. In the weeks since my prayer time with Jenny, it was as if I had forgotten the miracle work God had begun in my heart. There I was again, with a near stranger and our mutual best friend, inviting me into grace and out of lies.

"Bridget, there's also this other image I got when we were listening," Kaylyn said before we finished our prayer time. "I don't know if this is significant for you, but I saw you sitting on a dock, the weather was beautiful, and the sun was shining on your face. Does that mean anything to you?"

I cried happy tears and told her yes! God was reminding me that he has made me new, and not to forget the good work he was already doing in my life. This would become normal in every transition and hard season—God reminding and teaching me as I forgot his goodness and continued to live in my old ways instead of his new ones.

I long to be Mary. Sitting on the dock with Jesus, sun shining all around, rather than rushing about my own business. To revel in his presence instead of frantically worrying whether everything is taken care of. Mary knew the best place to be, and she made sure to find herself there. Even when good things like amazing friends and fulfilling community are hard to come by, community with Jesus cannot be taken away. Being with him is a good portion. It is necessary.

Pilgrimage Moment: Statio

Here's our first whisper of *holy aloneness*. Jesus invites us to sit at his feet and learn from him. This is a pilgrimage practice too—taking small moments with Jesus. Saint Brigid, one of the patron saints of Ireland, was known for taking contemplative pauses between transitions throughout her day. She had a lot of reason to because her life was full of service to those in need and hospitality to strangers. She spent her life caring for the earth and for the poor. She needed moments with Jesus.

This practice is called *statio*. It's a time to center yourself, connect with the Divine, and embrace the moment for exactly what it is. Statio serves to keep us from rushing ahead into sin, or letting another tentacle of brokenness win, or missing something God might want to teach us in the in-between.

Chances are, you've had a different experience of community than mine, so let's have a statio moment of our own.

Take stock of your life in this present moment. Are you aware of your unhealthy patterns and wrong beliefs? Do you have the kind of community and relationships that make it safe to step into spiritual growth and healing? Who are the fellow pilgrims walking alongside you on this journey?

In the next chapter I'll talk about what happens when we don't feel like there's a fellow pilgrim in sight. But before you move on, practice statio and say a prayer to God asking for the type of safe community that will help you see yourself, make space for growth and healing, and then send you out into new adventures.

4

COMMUNITY PART TWO: WHEN YOU DON'T HAVE IT

When do we learn how to be good friends? Shouldn't that be a required class in school? I know I just waxed poetic about the best friend group I've had in my life, but that was a holy and wonderful fluke. Most of life is not like my year on the Laughtern team. Most adult friendship is tricky, and we don't know what we're doing.

Apart from having shared hobbies, programs, and projects, we can struggle to form robust community and healthy relationships. Even when you have everything stacked in your favor, friendships can come up short.

That was what happened to me when I moved to Flagstaff. There was so much potential waiting there for me. I was living with one of my college friends, Megan, who is a fun, community-oriented, and adventurous woman, and we had amazing roommates. My InterVarsity staff team at NAU was big, and the students involved seemed like so much fun. And, to top it all off, my older brother Anthony had moved there a year before to plant a church with his wife, Jessica, and a bunch of their friends from college, and they were expecting their first child. I was going to be an aunt.

The first week I arrived in town, Jared and John, both student leaders in their fifth year, invited me for burritos. Many of the students had heard of me and wanted to welcome me; my reputation preceded me. When I rolled up to the restaurant, I saw them and a giant poster they made with a funny cutout of my face that read "WELCOME TO FLAGSTAFF BG!" I felt so loved.

Even though I was well-received by the students and bonded quickly with my roommates, community didn't really work out the way I hoped. The staff team wasn't close like my Laughterns. They had their own conflict, and I was stepping into the middle of a weird dynamic. I also thought I could seamlessly transition into my brother's church community, but those relationships didn't form into more than quick hellos after service on Sundays.

This was my first experience of how hard it is to maintain and foster quality friendships in adulthood. All I wanted was friends, but for some reason Flagstaff had meager offerings for me in that department. I had friends all around me and even family there, but I didn't have consistent and intentional community with them. As a new person in town, I would have benefited from more hospitality like I received from Jared and John, but it didn't often come my way.

Being a single person and an extrovert, this was especially hard for me. I've always struggled with asking for what I want and need from people. I already felt a little slighted by the lack of welcome from my peers, so how could I risk more rejection by asking people to be my friend?

Rejection.

There's no pain like experiencing rejection from a friend or going through a friendship breakup. As quickly and easily as they come into your life, friends can disappear, sometimes without a word of explanation. More of the heartbreak in my life has come from conflict with friends than from romantic interactions.

The more we experience pain from our friendships, the shier we can become to try again, especially when life gets difficult. In the face of rejection, it's easy to feel the temptation to throw in the towel and isolate ourselves for a while. Also, depending on your personality, making new friends may feel like a chore, requiring more energy than you feel you can muster.

Adulthood is a great time to learn how to be a good friend. Being single sets you up to say yes to invitations, and time is on your side—you have so much space to build beautiful friendships. Friendship is also a great context for learning how to be a faithful disciple of Jesus. Consider what Scripture says about our relationships with each other:

- "A friend loves at all times, and a brother is born for a time of adversity" (Proverbs 17:17).
- Jesus says, "My command is this: Love each other as I have loved you. Greater love has no one than this: to lay down one's life for one's friends" (John 15:12-13).
- "Be devoted to one another in love. Honor one another above yourselves" (Romans 12:10).

In the kingdom of God, the requirements of a good friend are high. We are commanded to love each other in a way that sets aside our own agendas. These verses invite us into a deeper level of commitment: devotion, steadfast love, sacrifice. Wouldn't you love to have friends like that? Wouldn't you love to be a friend like that?

Jesus was. He invites us into this kind of friendship because he lived it out. During his ministry he had twelve close friends, spent many meals at dinner parties, and brought the best wine to weddings. He approached and befriended people no one else would; he touched the untouchables, gave them time and attention, wept with them, forgave them, and restored their social standings. Jesus was the best friend to everyone who received his friendship.

Too often we let our fears of being hurt get in the way of laying down our lives for others or receiving this kind of sacrificial love. No doubt, you will get hurt when you take a risk on deep friendship and intentional community.

I've been stood up by friends, blocked without explanation, mistreated, manipulated, used, called names, betrayed, abandoned, neglected, taken advantage of, and on and on. After all I've been through, I could justify spending the remainder of my years alone in a cave on a mountainside somewhere. While that doesn't sound half bad, I'm still here, out in public, learning to pray for new friendships in my life with each passing year and for my current ones to grow and be more fruitful.

In the hardest seasons of friendship, I remember that Jesus knows what it's like to be hurt by his friends too, maybe to an even worse degree. Judas betrayed him into the hands of his murderers, and when he was on trial and was crucified, the rest of the disciples scattered. His friends abandoned him, those he had spent the previous three years pouring into, teaching, and loving. He transformed their lives and identities, but at the first sign of trouble, they were gone.

It's not just that Jesus can identify with my heartbreak over broken friendships that comforts me. It's that he still went to the cross and gave "his life as a ransom for many" (Mark 10:45). He knew he would be abandoned. He knew he'd be alone in the worst trial of his life. But resurrection life was more important to him than protecting himself—and he could have protected himself! But we were more important to him than his own life, body, and reputation. He had to die so we could live in that eternal resurrection life.

It's in this new life that we can have hope for redemption and reconciliation in our relationships—with God and each other. Jesus is the best friend that teaches us all how to be the best friend to others. As followers of Jesus, we should be the best at friendship. We should see that self-protection has no partnership with resurrection life.

IS IT WORTH IT?

Rejection is not the only thing that can keep us isolated and complacent in our relationships. There are so many excuses that keep us too busy to say yes to that taste of kingdom friendship. We have everything we need to entertain us at home: our devices and games and shows. And our calendars are filled with things we think will produce better outcomes for our checkpoints of adulthood, such as career opportunities and romantic relationships.

But isn't this the picture we're given for our twenties? That professional development and marriage are proof you're winning at adulthood? This attitude feels prevalent among young singles. And because of this, we miss out on one of our most vital needs as humans—community. We usually let our nonromantic relationships go to the wayside either because we assume they will work themselves out or because they're too hard to make happen.

Sometimes, we won't wade very deep into the waters of community before heading back to the shore of romantic partnership. Putting all our eggs in the marriage basket feels easier than developing vibrant and robust community. All metaphors aside, even today as a single woman in her early thirties, this still feels true.

I can hardly go to the grocery store at times without romanticizing a meet-cute with the bearded, tatted guy in the produce section. I have been so conditioned to find a partner that I have to do mental gymnastics to see handsome, unmarried men as friends first. It's not my reflex to view them as potential friends.

As embarrassing as this is to admit, I know it's common. We uplift romantic potential and interactions so much that we end up objectifying one another rather than seeing each other as humans worthy of platonic love. I feel it happening to me all the time too. And it's disheartening. It dims my vision for having quality community in my singleness.

For my friend Pieter though, he has cast all barriers aside to pursue lived-in, lifelong community with his roommates, who belong to the Nashville Family of Brothers. The group of men live together, eat together, pay their bills as a household, go on retreats and vacations together, and even regularly renew their covenant as a family of brothers. Pieter hopes to have a family of sisters come together to do the same thing in the near future. He takes seriously his calling to kingdom singleness and lives it out in an inspiring and encouraging way. His experience of growing up gay in the evangelical church led him to this place, creating deep community and thriving places of belonging for other LGBTQ+ people in the church.

While this picture of community is beautiful, it comes with its own risks and hardship, as with any family dynamic. The greater point is that Pieter and his brothers keep saying yes because the goodness of that chosen family far outweighs the drawbacks. I want to argue that communities like Pieter's are rare, but I don't think they are. People make commitments to nonromantic chosen family all the time; we just don't often hear about them in our heteronormative evangelical circles.

In fact, we could learn a lot from queer communities about deep friendship. For a people who have been alienated, abused, oppressed, and ignored by society and the church, countless stories portray deep love and support for one another when a healthy biological family wasn't available to them. I see glimpses of kingdom community in the tenderness, intentionality, acceptance, and loyalty of many friendships among queer people.

I long for all people of God to have that. Truly, this is what Jesus modeled for us with his community of disciples: They were all from the same people group, but they came from so many different perspectives. They held different opinions and experiences and had every reason to not want to be around one another. But the invitation to follow Jesus came with a commitment to one another too. As they watched the way Jesus loved, accepted, and made space for people, all their preconceived ideas about community were turned upside down.

The best investment of our energy for our whole lives is in our relationships with others. It's the foundation on which we can learn to love like Jesus and be loved back. More than our careers, more than our romantic endeavors—both can be ever-changing and temporary—friendship is what we were made for. You don't take your careers or marriages into eternity with you, but you can take your friends.

CAPITALIZING ON MY SINGLENESS

Often in new evangelical churches, I've heard sermons from married male pastors in their twenties and thirties talk about singleness in the same way:

You have all the time in the world to do kingdom work, since you're not married with a family.

This is their response to Paul's exhortation to single people in the Corinthian church to stay unmarried so they can have an undivided focus on God. Let's spend a moment here.

> I would like you to be free from concern. An unmarried man is concerned about the Lord's affairs—how he can please the Lord. But a married man is concerned about the affairs of this world—how he can please his wife—and his interests are divided. An unmarried woman or virgin is concerned about the Lord's affairs: Her aim is to be devoted to the Lord in both body and spirit. But a married woman is concerned about the affairs of this world—how she can please her husband. I am saying this for your own good, not to restrict you, but that you may live in a right way in undivided devotion to the Lord. (1 Corinthians 7:32-35)

Elsewhere in this chapter, Paul makes it pretty clear that this isn't law, but his Spirit-filled advice. He repeats a couple times that time is short; following Jesus was costly in its own way in that time and place. It could get them arrested and killed. Being unattached was the better option if they might lose their life for being Christians. On the other hand, the invitation to stay single and celibate in Corinth was countercultural in a city known for its religious prostitution. Single Christians would stick out like a sore thumb there. For the Corinthians, following Jesus came with extra risk and weight that we don't feel as deeply in our current Western context.

I love Paul's exhortation to stay single, but the interpretations I hear in church land far from his point. In these sermons, I hear, "Do more, be more, serve more, give more." This invitation sounds more like the capitalistic culture we live in than what Paul was getting at here, which is that being able to focus fully on God was the best option for anyone who could. However, instead of being encouraged in our devotion to God as singles, we hear, "Give more of your time and energy for the church, since we married people don't have it."

Even though I quite literally use my work hours for the "Lord's affairs," this messaging has never sat well with me. In these sermons, my time and energy were still being compared to married people and parents. As if they would be doing so much more for the church if they weren't in their relationships or families. (And don't get me wrong, that might be true . . . but we'll never know, will we?) It's a privileged stance to tell single people that they must be doing more for God with their apparent extra time and energy. And how dehumanizing to spend a sermon about singleness on telling single people that their call is to work harder.

Many single people live in survival mode, and the last thing on their minds is their free time. Some people have to work multiple jobs to afford their living situations, giving them no time for community or service. Some people are just alone in their lives—they don't have family or community showing up to support them. It shouldn't be this way, but that's the reality at times. The last thing these single people deserve to hear from church leadership is a beg for more volunteers. To be honest, it's just a poorly placed ask.

I would have loved to have a more robust experience at church and in my community, but my time in Flagstaff had notes of injustice. At one point I was working three part-time jobs to afford living there because I never got fully funded for ministry. And since my social and family life came up short, I leaned into my career. I used all my stovetop burners for InterVarsity and put the rest of my life in a little pot off to the side for later. I think that when you're young and single it's easy to give all of yourself to only those aspects of your life that feel full. My career in ministry felt like the most worthwhile thing, where I found the most joy and satisfaction. I was tired of trying so hard in all the other areas of my life.

My supervisor recognized that I was spending a lot of my energy working, and not enough time resting. He knew that if I continued in this pattern, I would not last long in ministry. So, he encouraged me to spend regular time in silence and solitude. And believe me, I tried. He let me borrow this brilliant book, *Invitation to Solitude and Silence: Experiencing God's Transforming Presence*, which helps readers practice being still and hearing God's voice.

But it was really uncomfortable for me. I didn't want to fix my attention on God. I wanted distraction because I knew that God would not only offer me unconditional love (which I still wasn't convinced I deserved), but also have me face more deep wounds that he wanted to heal. So, I neglected to press into the silence and solitude. Although I was using my time and energy for kingdom work, I'm not sure my attention was fixed on God. I was coping poorly. Why would I want to press into all those hard things when I could give my energy and intention to my job?

So, I get it! I get why we avoid the hard stuff that takes a lot of work, risk, and learning. It's easy to ignore the difficult stuff and press into only what's going well.

God is faithful to not let us remain that way. He saw me and my struggle more deeply than I could. Although he was patient and gentle with me, he was merciful to create space for me to address some deeper wounds, even while I was running around distracting myself.

"I WISH I HAD A HUSBAND"

The second year I lived in Flagstaff, things were a little chaotic in my job, but I found out early on that I would be returning to Tucson the following year to my alma mater. I had committed to five years at NAU, but I was getting to return to my beloved city early, after three years of being away. Suddenly, everything seemed so much more exciting.

One night, I was at my brother's apartment while he and Jessica were at a party to which I hadn't been invited. Even a year and a half in, I was the free babysitter while my brother and sister-in-law enjoyed the community that I desperately wanted. I told myself at least I had Anthony and Jessica as my family; they were sort of forced to let me be a part of their lives. Besides, I was too excited about my future to let it bother me too much. Or so I thought.

Anthony and Jessica had driven separately to the party that night, and he was the first one home. He came in and immediately turned on a basketball game. I wanted to wait around to say hi to Jessica, but she was taking her time. I hadn't told

Anthony about my Tucson news yet, so I attempted to strike up a conversation with him.

He and I have had a strained relationship for a long time. Growing up, he was my bully. He didn't like me very much, and nothing I did could really change that. I was relieved when he got more serious about Jesus in high school, and as he got older, he also felt called into ministry. We are very alike. We share a lot of main personality traits, as most siblings do, but it's like we have completely different dispositions. I am sunny and warm and dorky. Anthony is skeptical, witty, and always has something up his sleeve. I'm a little too mushy for his taste. And at times, he's a bit too sarcastic for me.

I had moved to Flagstaff with reservations about our relationship but with hope that we'd get a chance to work on it. With my departure approaching, time was running out for progress in our relationship.

"Anthony, did Jessica tell you about my news?" I struck up the conversation.

"What news?" he said in a monotone voice, with his eyes fixed on the TV screen.

"I'm moving back to Tucson after this school year. I get to do staff at U of A—my dream!"

"No, she didn't tell me." He still didn't look at me.

"Yeah, I'm really excited. I feel like God's answering my prayers."

"That's cool."

I didn't know if the Suns game was really that important, or if he didn't know how to interact with me, but I felt so deflated from our small chat. He didn't seem excited for me or proud of me. So instead of waiting for Jessica to get back, I decided to leave.

It was mid-December, and it had snowed a few days prior, so the sidewalks were icy outside. Two-and-a-half years in snowy mountain towns still had this desert child acting super cautious. It's hard to flee an awkward interaction when the ground is slippery. Sure enough, just as I approached my car, I slipped and hit my knee really hard.

I got up and hobbled to my car, got in, shut the door behind me, turned on the engine, and began to weep. At first, I thought it was the shock of the pain. But then, without a thought, a sentence escaped my sobbing lips.

"I wish I had a husband!"

Whoa. Where did that come from? I thought. Sometimes, physical pain is the only thing that can reveal our deep emotional pain.

Ever since my internship year, I had been taking a closer look at the ways that my childhood relationships with my family members had impacted me. God used my coworkers Chris and Kosmos to show me what true brothers can look like, which in turn gave me vision and hope that my relationship with my own brother could be restored. Jessica spent many years encouraging me and holding that hope for me too.

In that moment in the car, I was seeing the impact our relationship had on me. My desire for Anthony's support, attention, and approval quickly translated into a longing for a solution: a husband. As if having a husband would cover all wrongs: negate the fact that I felt so unloved by my grown-up brother. As if it would prove to me and to Anthony that I was worth loving.

Thank God that's not how things work! God has better solutions and greater invitations than we have for ourselves. Had I been married then, I still would have had to deal with my emotional pain and wrong beliefs that I was unlovable and unworthy of kindness. In fact, that would have been hard to navigate in a marriage anyway! God is so kind that his invitation was for restoration and wholeness in my relationship with my brother instead of the distraction of another man's love for me. That night in the car, I knew this would have to be addressed somehow. But I also knew that it would take God to do it.

Not much later, one of my students who had a great relationship with her older brothers encouraged me to talk to Anthony about our relationship with honesty. I was really scared, but when a student you're supposed to be discipling schools you, you take their direction.

That spring, I was invited to staff my first-ever global program in China. I hadn't had the chance to participate in one of these cultural and language exchanges during college, so I was eager to experience this. I went into my final semester in Flagstaff with so much to look forward to and consider. Anthony had traveled to China for similar programs three times before. So I asked him to have dinner with me to talk about how to best prepare for my trip. He obliged.

It wasn't China that I really needed to talk about. After a while of swapping ministry stories, I got up the nerve to bring up my feelings to Anthony.

"Anthony, I just want to say sorry for making it hard to be my brother." I had no clue how to start this conversation, so that was the best I could come up with.

I had spent so many years with walls up and distrust of him that I knew he was afraid to be himself around me, in case he hurt my feelings (which happened a lot). We were each other's most difficult triggers. I told him I didn't want it to be that way anymore. I braced myself for his response, but he wasn't defensive.

Anthony put his sunglasses on, even though we were indoors and the sun had already set. His eyes were welling up with tears. "Bridget, if I've never said sorry for bullying you growing up, I am sorry. It's one of my biggest regrets."

That was the first time I remember him apologizing like that. I almost couldn't believe it.

"I forgive you, Anthony. And I'll keep working on it. It had a deeper impact on me than I'd like to admit."

We talked for a while about a few ways that we could try better in the patterns we often found ourselves in. It was a beautiful release, a new taste of freedom.

Anthony and I are still working on our relationship today. I called him while writing this book to ask him what he thought. He was very honest about his experience with me, and he told me that he's committed to our relationship getting better. We are learning to support and accept each other as adults. I still hope we can learn to be better siblings to one another.

Family is always hard as an adult, but when you are single, it is still the most important relational unit. Being single means you haven't created a new family yet; you are still primarily someone's child or sibling, if you're lucky enough to have family! I had no plans to wade into the choppy waters of my issues with family and community. But God had other plans for me in this weird and awkward time of singleness. I didn't feel secure, seen, or like there was space for me, but God made space for new risk, self-awareness, and wholeness.

God has other plans for you too. Your family and childhood wounds may be deeper and more difficult than mine. Or, you may be unaware of the ways your formative years have impacted you. Either way, the invitation into risk, self-awareness, and wholeness is there for you too. We are not meant to remain in ignorance and broken relationships as people of God. There's always more for us.

At the end of my time in Flagstaff, God invited me to something much deeper than the limited life I was living, pouring all of myself into my career. He wanted me to turn all my burners on and get a variety of dishes cooking. God wasn't going to let me leave behind the other areas of my life just because they weren't going my way. We were going to make a feast of my life!

Pilgrimage Moment: Giving and Receiving Hospitality

Pilgrims aren't meant to see themselves as individual units but as together on the journey with others. And we need each other. Giving and receiving hospitality is an important practice in pilgrimage.

Now, some of us are better at one or the other—giving hospitality or receiving it. Which one are you better at? I'm really great at the first and terrible at the second. Pride wells up in me when I am vulnerable and need someone's help. I hate asking for it. But I could host parties, initiate, invite people over, and make them food *all day*! Letting myself be taken care of and loved? Much harder.

But this is what relationships are: giving *and* receiving. Not one or the other. Too much of one and not enough of the other creates imbalance in our relationships. There's a lot of lopsidedness out there. In what ways can you grow in hospitality? How can you start to see yourself as a pilgrim who gives and receives hospitality more equally?

Hint: the bonus content might help you with this.

As you grow in your hospitality, you may see that your experience and vision for deep, vibrant, and robust community grows too. I hope it does!

Bonus Content: Tips on Hospitality

Get excited. This is the one time I'm going to do this: give some direct advice. This isn't a self-help book and I'm no expert, but I have learned a lot about fostering community and healthy friendships in my short life, and I want more of that for us.

So here are some tips:

- Know yourself. What do you need? What do you want? What's your capacity? Do the people around you have capacity to be the type of community you need?
- Look around at what you *do* have. In certain seasons you may have a handful of friends who haven't gone anywhere. Or friends who would be there for you in a moments' notice. Sometimes we overlook certain friendships when our expectations aren't being met in other places.
- Don't settle for toxic friendships either. It won't take long for you to recognize patterns in others who only take in relationships and never give. If you can tell that boundaries are broken routinely, and that it is more than just a bad season for your friend, feel released to walk away. At times, we are willing to settle for bad friendships because those people are nearby, and they make themselves physically available to us. But bad friendships can negatively affect your mental health, so don't do that to yourself.
- Long-distance friendships are also worth it. We have no excuses these days not to stay in touch with our people if they want that! Write letters. Use technology.
- Don't skip things like church or small group. Be consistent with your opportunities to build relationships.

- Don't take things personally. Other people's behavior is not a reflection of your worth. If you sense that you've warranted some type of behavior from your friends, ask for feedback. Keep the communication open. If they don't want to explain themselves, you have to respect that, even if you don't understand. It's not about you.
- Practice gratitude daily. Thank God for what you have had, what you currently have, and God's presence in your life.
- Ask your friends to show up for you. This is the hardest for me. It feels like death because I've been let down so many times. But if you don't ask, chances are, you won't receive.
- Spend some concentrated time fostering new relationships in your life. Take risks and invite people out for coffee or over for dinner.
- Throw a party in your own style: an intimate party, a big party, a game night, a dinner party.
- Don't limit yourself! There are potential friends everywhere you go. Is there a hobby you want to get into? Take a class, invite a classmate to drinks afterward. Crosscultural friendships are so good too!
- Be intentional about who you live with. Start talking with other single friends about spending an intentional year together in community.
- Have meals with people.
- Have fun with people. You need to be laughing in this life!

5

WHY AM I STILL SINGLE?

In 2015, I thought I had somehow stumbled into my dream life. I was finally moving back to Tucson, one of the world's greatest cities, to do ministry at my alma mater after three years away. Before Tucson though, was our global program in China.

These programs include bonding with the Chinese students by practicing English and playing fun conversation games. One of these simple games involved taking turns pulling questions out of a hat and answering them for the whole room to hear. I went last.

I pulled:

What is the one thing missing in your life?

Yeesh.

"Well, probably a husband," I answered reluctantly.

The room full of students broke into a collective "aww."

"I have everything I ever wanted," I explained. "My dream job, wonderful experiences, great friends, a home, a car, all the food and clothes I could ever need. All that seems to be missing is a husband."

It felt silly to admit, but at the time, it also felt true. Most of my life I've felt this way. On that particular trip, I found myself really annoyed about my singleness in the first week. It may have had something to do with wishing that I had intimacy with my teammates already, but I couldn't help but feel my lack. I wished I had a husband there with me, enjoying the trip, processing the day's events, laughing and crying and praying together. That would be stellar.

Instead, I was roomed with a student. My directors, also both single staff workers around my age, wisely placed me with a student rather than let her room alone. In so many ways, I felt stuck in between: I was on staff but rooming with a student. I was in between cities that I lived in. I had just left one season and was entering the next. I had so much anticipation that this next season could be the one in which I meet my husband.

One night, I decided to pray about it. I was feeling so alive doing my job that I wondered, why even bother with marriage? Why do I want it so badly when I could live such a great life alone anyway? So, I took to my journal. I was lying on my belly on my twin bed, my roommate reading in hers. It was peaceful. After thanking God for my teammates and jotting down some wise words one of them shared, I wrote:

"So. It's true. I haven't fully surrendered my desire for a husband to you. I have held out hope that you would answer this prayer but I'm mad that you've waited so long to answer. What is your answer?"

At that moment, I decided I would just listen. So, I put my pen down, buried my face in my hands, and waited to hear from God.

Wait more.

That phrase kept repeating in my mind, nothing else around it, nothing else distracting me. In frustration, I said to God, "You know, I'm going to wait for you to say more than that, because how is that a new one? And isn't this the point? I don't want to wait more." Again, I put down my pen and covered my face to let God speak.

Then I saw an image in my mind, and this is what I wrote in my journal:

"I see a long stone staircase with more steps ascending—it doesn't seem to end. But I continue on the course and greenery is coming into view. My answer is on its way."

I didn't know what to think of this weird image and word from God but I knew it was him because it was vibrant and very real. I can actually still see it in my mind. As I climbed the steps, I was fatigued and annoyed, but hopeful when I saw I was nearing the top.

Even though it was a better response than "wait more" and a very clear image, I was annoyed by how fortune cookie-esque the whole thing was. "My answer is on its way?" What the heck does that even mean?

I was ready to move on, so I wrote:

"Can you help me lay down this desire at the foot of your cross so I may see my heart bowed and you resurrect it if you will?"

It feels vulnerable to share my prayer journal entry with you, but in the words of the pop singer Demi Lovato, this is real, this is me.

I remember this version of me at twenty-five years old: loving life, annoyed with her one big unanswered prayer, and feeling ashamed about it. I kind of hated myself for wanting to be married so badly. Why did I want something that God so clearly didn't want for me yet?

I understand now what twenty-five-year-old Bridget did not: It's okay to want to be married; it's okay to want love and

partnership. God made us that way. It's okay to want something you don't know you will ever have.

Every year since our internship in Boulder, the Laughterns
have tried to spend one weekend together catching up,
bonding, and seeing new things. Our reunion. One year, we
started a tradition of sharing and praying with one another. It
came at just the right time with the people I trust most. Two
years in a row, I felt safe enough to share that I was still so
frustrated at God in my singleness. I must have been very
transparent because Daniel saw right to the heart of the
matter. He encouraged me to let go of any shame I felt about
my desires. He reminded me with kindness and grace that
these desires are beautiful and God given. And he did it
without idealizing marriage. He wasn't uplifting marriage to
be a higher experience than singleness. He just wanted me to
know that in this case, it's totally okay to want what I want.

I wanted a relationship in which I was likely to experience
love, intimacy, growth, connection, and partnership—and I'm
over here saying, "Stop wanting that, Bridget. That's selfish of
you, Bridget. That's unholy of you."

What?! Of course I want that! Now, it makes more sense to
me. Marriage is a beautiful thing. I can want a beautiful
thing. Most of the things I want are beautiful. What was
stopping me from thinking it was okay for me to desire this
one beautiful thing?

My singleness has often been a sweet invitation out of the
culture and value systems of the Christianity I grew up in. I had
to unlearn a lot of things to find freedom in my life with Jesus.

American evangelicalism in the 1990s and 2000s said,
"Suffer, suffer, suffer . . . Thou shalt not want . . . anything, ever,
at all. It's the eleventh commandment, haven't you heard?" I

also heard direct and indirect messages about what I shouldn't want as a woman—namely sex. Therefore, wanting anything adjacent to sex (including marriage) seemed wholly unholy. In this culture, women are typically defined as the objects of desire, not the ones desiring.

Yikes. This is wild, isn't it? I am such a desirous person. God made me that way. He made me so romantic. I long and ache for love and romance in all its forms. And for all my singleness, God has delivered them in so many ways. God isn't the one telling me I cannot want the things I want. He's comfortable with our wanting.

I wasn't. Thus, the bedtime journaling. Back to the story at hand. . . .

After that holy and frustrating moment with the Lord, I had a wonderful summer in China. I loved the people, the food, and the way that God was the same there as he is at home. I completely forgot about that journal entry. I nearly forgot all about my longing for a husband. This seems often true: when life is full and exciting, contentment is easy to come by. When we are distracted from our longings by other wonderful things, those longings don't seem so important. It's kind of nice.

I felt like so much of my life was working out. I was getting so many things I wanted, and I got to add world travel to the list. It's like all this good fortune was validation that I was headed in some sort of correct direction with my life—signs of purpose and wholeness and value. We do this too, in our humanity: we like to look for signs that we are doing something right.

Even regarding singleness, we tell each other that you can do it a right way so that you'll end up with a spouse. I have heard from people that "it's when you least expect it" that your future spouse will come knocking. I knew that wasn't true because many, many of my friends never stopped expecting it and easily found themselves married. I have heard that only when you are "fully content in the Lord" is when he will give you a spouse. As if a spouse is a reward for contentment. And as if any of my married friends had achieved that level of nirvana right before meeting their spouse. I knew that wasn't true because for me, there have been so many moments and seasons of contentment in my life, where I felt no want, but my husband was nowhere to be found.

That may have been why I was so annoyed with my single-ness. I was content, I was living my best life, so where was my husband? Or where was my clear call to a lifetime of cel-ibacy? I was clearly misguided by all the bad theology I'd been given. None of these pieces of advice were affirmed by Scripture. None of these things aligned with what I knew about how the kingdom of God works. Of course I found myself in this internal battle!

Either way, I let the adventure of my China trip distract me from this issue. Once again, God was merciful to work out my issues, distracted or not. During the last week with our friends, playing that question game, all the feelings came rushing back.

Why couldn't I just be happy with what I had? I really had so much. Why couldn't I just give it a rest? "Give it a rest, Bridget! You do the Lord's work! Focus. Focus. Focus."

But I couldn't focus.

As part of our team debriefing time, we went to the Great Wall. Hikes with friends can be such a toss-up for me. If it's one friend, I know they won't leave me behind. If it's a whole group, then surely someone will stay with me. But honestly, when we got there, I knew this was going to be a tough climb for me. I knew I'd be left behind. I let everyone know, and, I'll admit, I came in with an already defeated attitude. Why couldn't we take the gondola like everyone else? I was for sure going to be the last to the top.

I was right. I had neglected to confirm my exercise-induced asthma for years. I've lived my whole life trying to convince myself and others that I am *so* not a nerd. I couldn't have glasses *and* asthma. Nope. Not me.

Yes. Me.

So, there I was climbing seemingly never-ending ancient stone steps and one by one, I lost sight of all my teammates. Being one of the staff leaders doesn't make you a high priority for anyone, really. A little over halfway up, I was alone. Sure, there were other tourists, but I was alone. It was a really hard climb for me. I tried to stay positive and keep a steady pace, but the longer I was alone, the more frustrated I got.

"What if I never make it? What if I get up there and can't find anyone? It's not like they're waiting for me."

They weren't.

As time went on, I could tell that I started getting closer to the top, so I challenged myself to book it up the flight of steps in front of me. I braced myself and swiftly lifted my legs one after the other again and again until . . .

I just had to stop, and I hadn't made it to my goal.

In exasperation, I plopped down on a step. I was beet red, sweaty, tired, and alone. I could see the wall right up there, but I had no will to make it.

And then I got really angry. "Why am I alone? What's wrong with me? Why can I see it, but I'm not there yet? Why am I so easily left behind? Why is everyone there before me? Why am I such a wimp?" I could see the wall, but it felt so far away. I thought I should just head back down. No one would notice. No one would care.

It was rough. I swear, I almost stood up and started heading down, never to see the view from the Great Wall of China. But then I heard someone call my name.

"Bridge!"

My teammate Eli had come looking for me. I wasn't quite out of my anger yet. In fact, I was embarrassed to be caught in such a moment of weakness. He ignored my grumbling and negativity, helped me up, and somehow, we were on the wall in less than a minute.

It was almost comical. I ended up having a lovely time on the Great Wall that day. I wasn't alone. Someone had thought of me and came back for me. He spent time with me, took my picture for me. I don't think Eli knew what a gift that was to me after I threw that internal fit on the side of the mountain.

The next day we were in the thick of debrief and our afternoon activity was to individually chart the highs and lows of the past six weeks. At first, I was like, "How?" And quickly God reminded me about how I wrote in my prayer journal nearly every day that trip. So, I began to read. And then my heart came to a screeching halt only four entries in. I reread what I had written only a month before, and I realized that God had given me a vision and words for my experience on the Great Wall.

"I see a long stone staircase with more steps ascending—it doesn't seem to end. But I continue on the course and greenery is coming into view. My answer is on its way."

Again, I found myself lying belly down on a twin bed, hearing from God loud and clear. The day before, he had plucked me right out of the pages of my journal and put me on the Great Wall. I was floored, stunned, moved, freaked out. I don't know if he had ever spoken and acted this clearly in my life before that point. I couldn't believe it.

"Um, God are you kidding me? This was *yesterday*. You gave me a vision for something I was about to do?"

Yes. And remember yesterday? When you were mad and asking those questions?

"How can I forget?"

Well, do those questions sound familiar?

I thought back to yesterday: Why am I alone? What's wrong with me? Why can I see it, but I'm not there yet? Why am I so easily left behind? Why is everyone there before me?

Um, whoa.

Aren't those the same questions you ask in your singleness?

My mouth was agape, I nodded slightly, stunned.

I'm here to answer them, baby. First of all, Bridget, you are never alone (Isaiah 43:1-5). *Don't forget that. I am with you always* (Joshua 1:9). *Nothing is wrong with you. I made you well and I love you* (Psalm 139:13-14). *As for the rest, will you learn to trust me?*

"After that?! Will I trust you?! Uh, *duh!*"

A God who can teleport you from the pages of your journal to the side of a mountain is a God worth trusting.

Isn't God so merciful to get to the meat of the matter? I needed to know that I wasn't alone. That I was loved. That nothing is wrong with me. That my life is the exact one God wants for me right here and right now. How sweet of him not only to answer my heart's actual longings, but also to send a friend to come and get me. I felt so loved.

That day was just the beginning of me learning to trust and believe that what God spoke to me was true, that he was far more in control than I knew. The question was, would I continue to cling to these truths in my singleness as I moved back to Tucson for my supposed dream life?

Pilgrimage Moment: The Practice of Asking Questions

Growing up, I loved reading the Psalms. Every time I got to the emo ones though, where David questions God with "Where are you?" and "How could you do this to me?" I immediately felt dissonance. I could not relate. As a child, I was usually happy and didn't attribute anything difficult or unhappy to God.

And then I grew up a little. Life got harder. There were a lot of circumstances I wasn't okay with living through. My prayers calling out to God sounded a lot more like David's psalms of despair. Because who else should have to reckon with injustice or pain? Surely only God can. Coming to God with my questions has become more and more normal for me, especially when I'm unable to find answers elsewhere.

We can make asking questions a common practice in our spiritual walks. Whenever something doesn't sit right with you or you feel plagued by a certain issue, start asking questions. A lot of us grew up in a spiritual setting in which we were encouraged to believe and behave without question. But if you spend a little time in the Word, you see that people all over Scripture question God. They ask things like,

"What do you mean?"

"How am I supposed to do that?"

"What will they think?"

"Where are you?"

"Why are you letting this happen?"

"Why did you do that?"

In the case of my singleness, I kept coming up against the question of my longings: is it okay for me to want this? Is it okay for me to want marriage? If so, then why hasn't it happened yet? Why do I feel alone and unloved and unchosen? I had to ask or else I would go on believing wrong things that I was taught, directly and indirectly, by church leaders growing up.

Pay attention to what questions come up for you while we're on this pilgrimage together. Do you have the same questions about your singleness or different ones? Do you have a hard time believing the claims I make about God? Do you need your own experience with him?

Make time and space for that. Treat your questions like stones you can hold in your hands. How do they make you feel? How weighty are they? Sit with them for a while, undistracted. Are you willing to offer your questions to God with an open hand? Are there answers in Scripture?

I don't want to make it seem like hearing from God is so easy. It takes time and patience, and it can be uncomfortable. You also must learn to trust your hearing. The only reason I believe the things I have sensed from God is because they have been clear, affirmed, and in line with what Scripture says about his character and love for us.

I believe that God will be faithful to build trust with you in his answering, and that his answers will be far better than you could hope.

6

LONELINESS

"**Truly, truly, I say to you,** unless a grain of wheat falls into the earth and dies, it remains alone; but if it dies, it bears much fruit" (John 12:24 ESV).

In Tucson, I remained alone. Metaphorically, I was a grain of wheat, flying in the wind, unwilling to land, unwilling to die to my old patterns. I had a new chance to form community, make a feast of my life, and practice a deeper level of trust in God. But I didn't right away. And it's a shame too because God had done so much to reveal himself to me.

Luckily, I'm not the only one who has seen the glory of God and still questioned his ways. We see this in Mark chapters six and eight. The disciples follow Jesus' instructions to feed a crowd of five thousand, Jesus blesses what they have, and it multiplies to more than enough bread and fish for everyone there. This feeding miracle happens again a short time later. This time, the disciples ask:

"How can one feed these people with bread here in this desolate place?" (Mark 8:4 ESV).

They seem to immediately forget the first time they were in this situation. They weren't eager to see Jesus repeat the same miracle, but Jesus answers their question by satisfying thousands of people once again. Later in chapter eight, the disciples find themselves in a boat with Jesus, after the Pharisees had demanded a sign of him.

> The disciples had forgotten to bring bread, except for one loaf they had with them in the boat. "Be careful," Jesus warned them. "Watch out for the yeast of the Pharisees and that of Herod."
>
> They discussed this with one another and said, "It is because we have no bread."
>
> Aware of their discussion, Jesus asked them: "Why are you talking about having no bread? Do you still not see or understand? Are your hearts hardened? Do you have eyes but fail to see, and ears but fail to hear? And don't you remember? When I broke the five loaves for the five thousand, how many basketfuls of pieces did you pick up?"
>
> "Twelve," they replied.
>
> "And when I broke the seven loaves for the four thousand, how many basketfuls of pieces did you pick up?"
>
> They answered, "Seven."
>
> He said to them, "Do you still not understand?" (Mark 8:14-21)

After seeing Jesus provide for a multitude, the disciples, who were the hands and feet of the first feeding miracle, were still clueless. They were still worried about their own stomachs and neglected to recognize that the Savior of the World was right in front of them. Their trust in his miracles was short-lived, even though he had repeatedly shown himself to be trustworthy. Jesus was right to call them out because he didn't want them to be like the Pharisees or Herodians, who expected something different of their messiah.

I have been just like the disciples—gladly following Jesus, having a front-row seat to his miraculous ways in my life and others' lives, and yet still asking, "Where's the bread?"

This is exactly what landed me in urgent care a few months after I moved back to Tucson.

I'd so hoped Tucson would be a feast of life, but it had been a bit of a letdown. Loneliness started to creep in. I felt disappointed in my friends, my job, and my love life for not living up to my expectations. So quickly, too—only three months into my return, I had already thrown in the towel. Things were hard. I felt distant from the joy and hope I brought into this season. Great Wall Bridget felt far, far away. Where was the trust? Where was the hope in God's provision even when the journey got rough?

One afternoon, I borrowed a weed whacker from my coworker, deciding that, as a single gal and new homeowner, I could do my own yardwork. It wasn't a man's job. It was my job. Watch out, world. There I was, ready to prove to everyone that I didn't need anyone. At the time, I thought my attitude was good. In the face of my disappointment, it seemed like a healthy coping mechanism to lean into my independence.

After forty-five minutes of holding the loud, vibrating weed whacker, I'd had enough. I was done for the day. I patted myself on the back and told myself I would finish tomorrow. Later that evening, I was over at my coworker's house for a game night, but I felt really fatigued. All I wanted was to stretch out on their living room carpet and rest. As an extrovert, this was very odd behavior. The next morning, I felt even worse; my chest was heavy, my entire body ached, and my breathing was labored, so I took the day off work.

As I lay in bed that day, trying to retrace my interactions and figure out how I got sick, God told me plain and simple.

You have pneumonia. From weed whacking.

"No, no, no, God. You're silly. How is that even possible? This is just a quick cold. I'll feel better tomorrow. I always snap back after high doses of vitamin C and a day's worth of sleep."

But two more sick days passed, and I didn't get better, so I took myself to urgent care. The attitude of independence remained; I wasn't willing to ask one of my roommates to take me.

I told the nurse practitioner that I suspected I had pneumonia, even though I'd never had it before. Luckily, she took me seriously and had me get chest x-rays. I waited nervously for the results, and when she came back in the room, I knew just by the look on her face that God was right: pneumonia.

I immediately burst into tears. I was so embarrassed that I was responsible for this. I could have come in sooner. My pride caused this whole situation. After she called in my prescriptions, I got in my car, still crying and called my mom.

"Mom, I have pneumonia," I sobbed.

"Oh honey, I'm sorry. Are you okay? Do you want me to come down there?" she offered, just to comfort me.

"What would you even do?" I asked, feeling like a seven-year-old again.

She laughed. "Just stare at you while you recover."

"No, Mom, it's okay. I don't want to make you do that," I said, even though I kind of did.

"You know I would!" she offered again.

"I know. I just hate this, mom. This is exactly why I wish I was married. Then someone who is contractually obligated to take care of me could drive me to urgent care and then to the pharmacy to get my drugs. And do my yardwork for that matter!"

"What about your roommates or your friends?"

"It's too late, now, isn't it?"

"No, they can still get your prescriptions for you."

"I guess that's true. Okay. I'll try calling around."

I could tell that if my mom were in the same city, she would have helped me in a heartbeat. But there was no reason for her to rush down. I wasn't in imminent danger. And to be honest, that's never been our relationship. I'm the kid my parents don't have to worry too much about. She'll always land on her feet. She's capable. She's smart. She's a hard worker.

The irony of the situation was that I didn't really need to prove that I was so independent in the first place; people already thought this about me. And this thought process led to my demise.

The truth is, I am not that independent. I am not that much of an individual. I need people. And it shouldn't take until the point of desperation for me to call up a few friends last minute to help me when I'm down. I'm sad to report that in this case, my friends weren't available to help me, further reinforcing my attitude that I was on my own for this one.

Before moving to Tucson, I didn't have eyes to see that I had been functioning in scarcity. I looked at what I had and thought I was majorly lacking. Often, my idea of provision was in the form of a husband, rather than taking the risk to seek out the help and love of my community. This cycle of thinking would follow me everywhere I went if something didn't change. God's so great because he takes what we have and always makes more with it. He was ready to feed me the good stuff. The deep stuff. Real bread. God's invitation for me wasn't just to have a full life, but to also have freedom in my humanity as both a strong and needy person meant for more robust relational experiences.

As prideful as I was to remain in my patterns, I was in for a load of God's mercy.

WHO IS RESPONSIBLE FOR ME?

There I was, wearing all these different hats: friend, roommate, landlord, campus minister, and collector of part-time jobs I hated. I didn't feel like anyone cared about what was going on with me. I had very little money. I was past my capacity. I felt like the disciples, stuck in a boat, looking at the loaf of bread that is my life and wondering how I was going to get more. Even with Jesus in the boat with me, I was still left wondering: Who is taking care of me?

It sure wasn't me. I was ignoring me and my needs.

Just as a quick reminder, this is *my* story. Maybe you're not like me at all. What I do know to be true though, is that we all can be guilty of making it someone else's responsibility to take care of us. And a lot of times, we expect that to come in the form of a romantic relationship.

Historically, this makes sense, as for many decades, American women basically got married to survive. Before women could work at a livable wage, getting married was the most lucrative life choice. Women were not allowed to open a personal bank account without a male cosigner until the 1960s.[1] Society hasn't long been in favor of women being independent. Getting married meant you were covered. For men in these traditional roles, getting married meant being taken care of by their wives. She would make the home—buy things, cook, clean, and raise up the children while he was making money for all of it. This was the model of stability for a very long time.

Then things changed. Men went to war and women had to work. When the men returned, women felt empowered to continue working and another wave of the women's movement resulted. Bras came off, the average age of marriage rose and rose and rose, and society began to shift. Did our thinking shift, though?

In her book *All the Single Ladies*, Rebecca Traister describes women in the 1990s living in New York City taking care of each other and being taken care of by the city itself.[2] With the structures available in urban spaces, single women could thrive independently and advance in their careers. They didn't need to be married to live safe and flourishing lives.

These developments are only decades old, and both religious and secular schools of thought continue to perpetuate the ideas that single people are less valid in our society. Although the brunt of this belief falls on women, anyone can walk around believing that outside of a romantic relationship, we will not be taken care of or loved well. This narrow view of provision and care can lead to any number of poor coping mechanisms—self-neglect, in my case. Some people are driven into unhealthy relationships, often relationships that are built as temporary fixes, not built to last.

The truth is, when we are taken care of, our lives have a chance to flourish. If not a romantic partner, then who is responsible for our flourishing?

Ultimately, God is responsible. But so are you and your community.

In those first years living back in my favorite town, I had problems with all three. My problem was with me first. Secondly, my problem was with my community; because I was unwilling to admit to myself that I had any needs, I didn't ask for what I needed from my loved ones. Instead, I struggled and cried out to God, hoping he would magically snap his fingers and my problems would melt away.

None of that was working. I kept on in my ways, wondering when I would find another loaf of bread. The apostle John gives us more insight on what happened around the feeding of the five thousand in John chapter six. Jesus says, "I am the bread of life; whoever comes to me shall not hunger, and whoever believes in me shall never thirst. But I said to you that you have seen me and yet do not believe" (John 6:35-36 ESV).

I was having a hard time believing. I had seen Jesus do amazing things in my life, but I was still so hungry and thirsty for more and better. I couldn't see that God's way was more and better than mine. I was at an impasse. God's answer was to sweep in with his wild mercy, to let me know that if I kept doing things this way, I would keep being sick and disappointed. God's mercy is a reminder that while our ways will often lead to destruction, his ways lead to freedom. His invitation to freedom is ongoing.

I was a bit stubborn. Why was I like this? What had landed me here? My Octopus of Brokenness reared its ugly head.

DEPRESSION

Wearing many hats wasn't just a self-imposed reality for me. I found myself in a predicament at a student conference that same year I got pneumonia. When I showed up, the leaders asked me to attend a seminar at the same time as I was scheduled to lead another; there had been some miscommunication between the leaders. It stressed me out, but I tried to swing it. I didn't see another option.

That first night of the conference ran long. When I got back to my hotel room around 1:30 a.m., I realized my body was covered in hives from head to toe. I was so confused; it couldn't have been the Thai food I had that night, could it? I got the same thing I always get, and it was delicious. I hadn't had this kind of reaction to food before.

Bridget, you're stressed. God spoke in the quiet of the hotel bathroom as I stared down at my skin.

"What? No. I'm fine, I couldn't possibly have this bad of a reaction to my stress . . . it must have been the Thai, God."

No. It's your stress. You are stressed from head to toe.

This alarmed me because it was eerily familiar. Was God telling me *again* what was wrong with me, and I was *again* denying it?

Even so, I called my dad the next morning to get his medical advice. He is a registered nurse.

"Dad, is it possible to get hives from being stressed?"

"Well, yes, but could it have been something you ate?"

"I don't know, I had Thai food last night, but nothing different from what I've had before."

"Maybe they put something in it that you don't normally eat. Allergies can change over time, too. You should get the list of ingredients."

"Yeah, but Dad, I think it's stress. Not my curry."

"Really?"

"Yeah. God told me it was."

"Oh. Well, in that case, call me later today if your hives come back."

After the phone call, one of my Arizona teammates pulled me aside and told me that the leader of my seminar advocated for me in their morning staff meeting. He reassured me that I shouldn't have been expected to be two places at once. My hives flared up on my forearm as we spoke. As much as I wanted to appease him and say, "No, no it's fine," I could tell something deeper was at work. The One who whispered to me in the hotel bathroom had mercy to keep peeling back the layers.

Later that day, I called my dad back to let him know that I thought my hives might be a physical sign of a deeper emotional and mental issue. On the call, I admitted out loud for the first time that I was depressed. I was afraid to tell him because he often has a holy answer or Bible verse for every problem in life, rather than having a normal conversation. But I took the risk anyway.

"I think I'm depressed, Dad. You and Mom keep saying how I was never a sick child. I think all these physical ailments are my depression speaking out loud." I braced myself for whatever Scripture he had for me.

"Why are you depressed, honey?"

I was shocked at his tender response. A question. No judgment, no hesitation, just acceptance of my story. "I think it's because I feel so lonely."

"Really?"

"Yeah. Being single is rough, Dad. The older I get, the harder it feels. Who do I belong to? Who's gonna take care of *me*? I'm in charge of so much and then at the same time, I'm taken advantage of like at this conference. Or I'm not taken seriously because I'm not married, as if that's a symbol of maturity."

At the time, this is the answer I gave about my depression. Those words are how I felt, but I think depression is much more complicated. At the core of it though, I felt so alone.

"Oh, honey, I'm sorry. Look, marriage is hard too. I just want you to hear that. It's okay that you're single at twenty-six. I wouldn't trade your current situation for marriage because it's its own set of struggles. And you're not alone. Your mother and I will help you in any way you need us to. We are here for you."

I was moved at the words of wisdom and love coming from my dad. He didn't wash over my situation with holy platitudes; there, alone in my hotel room over the phone, I felt heard and seen. I was amazed. The burden lifted just a little. I knew I needed to keep taking risks to ask for what I wanted and needed, even if it felt costly. It was starting to feel costlier not to.

My depression helped me face some of the harder realities of my internal world. I'm a very external person; my whole perceived world happens outside of me. So, what happens when your external world is terrible? The internal world cries out for attention. And for me, this came in the form of pneumonia, hives, and later, a string of sinus infections. The more I neglected to face my internal world and deal with it in a healthy way, the sicker I got. I'm embarrassed to admit that this went on for about two years.

THE PRESENTING PROBLEM

My supervisor, Jon, who had been my InterVarsity campus minister in college, had a front-row seat to my suffering, and he offered the best help he had access to: Potter's Wheel. Potter's Wheel is a group counseling program here in Tucson that was developed by a couple named John and Patti Cepin. They lead a five-day intensive in which the group learns a theological framework of sin and personal development, and then sits in their stories together. Time spent "at the wheel" is an hour-long interview with Patti about what needs to be addressed right then and there in your life, followed by an hour of feedback from the group.

Yes. They watch and listen as you pour out your heart.

The week was life-changing for me. Until that point, I didn't have eyes to clearly see my dysfunction or the energy to change my patterns. I came face-to-face with my Octopus of Brokenness and started to see what the tentacles were made of:

I was a people pleaser of the highest degree.

I spent so much time and energy making everyone else happy, often at the expense of myself. I realized that in a way, I was conditioned to do this with the triple whammy of goals growing up: earn success, earn love, and earn salvation.

Children are poor interpreters of the messages and expectations they hear. But as a kid, being likable and successful felt like my ticket to getting loved. And for all that I did to earn it, it never felt like enough. It was a very lonely way to grow up. And remember my story with my dad in the charismatic church? I carried the weight of my own salvation around with me for most of my formative years.

Honestly, it could have been worse. I somehow avoided any number of disorders that could've easily developed in my psyche. But I was a cheery kid. I was happy to be alive in the sunshine of the desert. Even when hard things happened, I snapped back quickly.

I don't remember showing my anger very often though. I remember shoving it down, thinking it was invalid, didn't matter, wouldn't be helpful. So, I aimed to please. Less of me, more of everyone else. And it got bad. I let people walk all over me. I let them treat me poorly. I let them break boundaries all the time. I shouldered so many of their burdens that weren't mine to carry.

In hindsight, it's no wonder I idealized romantic relationships as an answer to my woes. It was the only type of relationship I could imagine in which you didn't have to earn anything. Theoretically, it was a relationship based purely on
mutual delight. Who wouldn't want that?

I also thank God I didn't end up testing that theory very
much in my young adulthood. I'm glad I didn't lay the burden
of my pain and bad patterns on a romantic partner. Instead,
Jesus was inviting me to come to him with my burdens to
trade them out for his light ones (Matthew 11:28-30). By the
time I showed up at Potter's Wheel, I was weary and heavy
laden. I needed rest.

The night before my turn "at the wheel," one of the partici-
pants shared about her unreconciled relationship with her
abusive brother, and something broke in me. I felt deep an-
guish. I couldn't stop crying. Terrible lies invaded my thoughts.
I tried to call my roommates and ask them that no visitors
come to the house that night, because I needed some alone
time, but one roommate said she was celebrating 18 months
with her boyfriend that night in our backroom in a fort she
had made for them. That was the last thing I wanted to come
home to, especially when I felt under spiritual attack. So, I
tried to ask her to celebrate on a different night. She didn't
understand. My other roommate called me to see what was up,
and I explained to her how I was feeling.

"I want to die, Kelly. I feel awful and I don't want to do this.
I want to go to bed and never wake up."

My depression was raging. Kelly was worried that I was sui-
cidal, but I wasn't. In my experience of depression, I just
wanted to escape. At worst, I wanted to die in my sleep, not by
my own hands. As a kind gesture and an act of peacemaking,

Kelly and our friend Danielie got me a hotel room for two nights. They wanted me to retreat, to have that safe space to be alone. It was a grace amid such chaos in my heart. Even when you're feeling the most violent loneliness, true solitude is the right remedy.

The next day, my turn came to face Patti, and talk through my "presenting problem." Despite the previous night being so difficult, it was still in my nature to outwardly pretend that there was no problem at all. I wasn't sure where to start, but because of our few days of built trust, Patti decided to start for me.

She asked, "Have you always been an angry person, Bridget?"

I was alarmed and defensive.

"What? No. I'm not angry. I'm hardly ever angry."

"Really? Then how were you feeling when your roommate built a fort in your home for her year-and-a-half anniversary without asking you? And how did you feel when she didn't want to respect your wishes to celebrate on another night?"

I thought for a moment. "Okay. Angry. Upset. Hurt."

"And how often do you feel that way?"

My heart dropped. *Oh no. All the time. And I have to admit this right now?*

"Okay. I guess I am an angry person. All the time," I said with a sigh.

"Let's talk about that."

We started talking about my anger and how it stemmed from unmet needs. That I do not stand up for myself, set boundaries, or communicate what I want and need very often. I lived in these roles: homeowner, team leader, landlord, campus minister, friend, and never laid out what I wanted, needed, and expected. I didn't feel like I deserved to, because

I thought it was my job to prove my value and lovability, not just to ask to be loved and valued. I knew all this stuff, but I wasn't really willing to accept it until sitting with Patti and my new friends.

I said that I missed Little Kid Bridget—you know, that starry-eyed one? Happy, believing in Jesus, brave, romantic. I felt so far from her. She used to burst out of bed with a song on her lips every single morning. That hadn't happened for me in a long time.

During the communal response time to my hour "at the wheel," Patti's husband, John, made an important observation. He told me that although I longed to be a little kid again—my childhood self—I couldn't. I wasn't her. I was grown-up. I was now Woman of God Bridget.

"What is Woman of God Bridget like?" he asked. "And I don't mean who you are right now in this moment, I mean who God made you to be. Do you think you know who that is?" He was asking me if I had eyes to see myself apart from these roles I've played in my life, apart from the ways I could benefit others.

It didn't take me long to answer. "She's strong. She's brave. She's prophetic. She's a leader." He nodded with every sentence.

"That's who you are. That's who you get to be now. You've matured into Woman of God Bridget and you can be her," he said. The rest of the room agreed. They prayed a blessing over me after those two hours, that I would leave there as Woman of God Bridget, no longer believing the lies of my childhood that I had to earn love and salvation, that I had to prove myself. There was a way that I was partnering with the enemy in believing such death over myself. So, Patti had me "break up with the enemy" and commit to cutting ties with those lies. Then she prayed something over me that scared me.

"Would that you never give anyone what they want ever again." These were types of prayers I had never prayed before. Patti was praying that I wouldn't keep returning to my cycle of people pleasing and validation because it wasn't bringing me love or freedom. It was keeping me trapped. Her bold prayer was to release me of the burden I brought to Potter's Wheel, one that I couldn't exactly name just a few days before.

Old Bridget was dying. Woman of God Bridget was being born again. God was merciful.

DRAWING BOUNDARIES

Returning home the next day, my roommate and her boyfriend were there, and they seemed worried about me. It was my first chance to be Woman of God Bridget, brave and strong, having needs, so I attempted to apologize and explain my situation. I apologized for not asking sooner for what I wanted and needed from them. They were at the house a lot, and it wasn't necessarily a problem unless I needed some space and quiet. In fact, my roommate had apologized for that numerous times, and I had pretended it didn't bother me.

My apology was met with defense. My roommate's boyfriend verbally attacked me in my own kitchen, and he told me not to respond—he silenced me, and my mouth went dry with anxiety. Eventually, my roommate stopped him and ushered him out of the house. We agreed to have a follow-up conversation.

That night, she and I made some boundaries for when he could come over. For having just been treated so poorly, the rules were very lenient, in my opinion. For the first time though, I was setting boundaries, asking for what I wanted and needed. And my roommate agreed.

Setting boundaries is one thing, reinforcing them is a whole other issue.

One night, I heard her boyfriend come over past our new curfew. He had clearly come to argue with her. Even though they argued in as hushed tones as they could manage, I could hear everything from my bedroom. I was fuming. It made me livid that they were willing to break the new rules for the sake of an argument, and I didn't like how he was treating her.

I sat in my bed and cried out to God, "Lord, see? This is a moment I wish I had a husband."

So badly, I wanted to have the bravery and authority to go stand in the doorway of my backroom and say to him, "Get out of my house. You are not welcome here like this." But I knew he wouldn't listen to me. So instead, I sat paralyzed in my bed, wishing for a husband.

"God, can you please make him leave in the next minute? I need you to be my husband! I need you to make him go!"

And what do you know? Thirty seconds later, I heard the back door open and shut. God had answered my prayer in less than a minute. Again, I was floored. (I'm realizing that I am often *floored* by God.) I started crying because I couldn't believe that God would come to my aid so quickly. I didn't even need to move from my bed!

All over Scripture, God is referred to as our husband (Isaiah 54:5; Hosea 2:16-19). His relationship with us is meant to be tender and intimate, as well as protective and mighty. It's easy to distance ourselves from God as a true husband. In my old patterns, I was unwilling to give God his rightful place in my life—the one who loves me unconditionally, the one who paid it all (so I don't have to spend my time earning a thing), and the one who longs to be close to me and take care of me every day. My husband.

I know this probably feels so cheesy. But God has undoubtedly shown himself to me as husband in many ways. Knowing I am covered, loved, and protected by my God helps me take bigger risks in my relationships with others because I won't be trying to earn something I already have.

Roommate relationships are hard to navigate for single Christians. I think there's an expectation of how we will act and treat each other as we live together, but we often disappoint one another in our humanness. It's hard to know if your roommates are committed to your well-being. I had failed my roommate by not communicating my expectations and boundaries early and often. Even if you do communicate well from the beginning and set up good boundaries and rules, they still might be broken. We are complicated creatures, maybe especially as Jesus followers. My roommates haven't always considered the relationships in our home a priority, an indication of their view on what living with other people means. Inviting people into deeper community and more meaningful relationship is always risky because sometimes, they don't want it.

I have always wanted it, though—deep community and meaningful relationships. In that season of my life, I didn't want to take the risks to ask for it even though I was painfully lonely. It was much easier for me to keep dreaming of a spouse that would come along and fix all my problems. I thank God that those dreams didn't come true at the time. I needed more. I needed the Bread of Life.

Jesus took my meager loaf of bread and began to multiply it into the rightful feast that he intended for me. This was the roughest period of my life, and I wouldn't relive it if you paid me. But it unveiled the wrong patterns and beliefs that kept me trapped and chained and thinking I was alone.

Loneliness is a great teacher, if you let it teach you.

Pilgrimage Moment: Listening Prayer

For this pilgrimage moment, let's place ourselves in the text. This is a listening prayer activity using Mark 8:14-18 (ESV):

> Now they had forgotten to bring bread, and they had only one loaf with them in the boat. And he cautioned them, saying, "Watch out; beware of the leaven of the Pharisees and the leaven of Herod." And they began discussing with one another the fact that they had no bread. And Jesus, aware of this, said to them, "Why are you discussing the fact that you have no bread? Do you not yet perceive or understand? Are your hearts hardened? Having eyes do you not see, and having ears do you not hear? And do you not remember?"

Jesus wants himself for the disciples. But they are having a hard time seeing clearly, even after witnessing miracles. He wants them to know him as their satisfaction, their protection, their Savior. Jesus wants the same for us.

Listening prayer can create space for us to receive from Jesus. This activity will take a little bit of holy imagination. Find a place to be alone, undistracted. Before we start, let's say a prayer to invite the Holy Spirit into the space.

"Holy Spirit, come. Open our eyes. Release our ears. Soften our hearts to receive from you."

Imagine yourself in the boat with Jesus and you have a loaf of bread. He asks you for it, but you cling to it tightly. Take a moment to consider what that loaf of bread is for you. What in your life leaves you with a scarcity mentality? What things are you tempted to cling to? Take a moment to listen for a word or an image.

Now, Jesus asks you for this loaf of bread again. Remember, he can multiply bread. When you're ready, in your mind's eye, hand your loaf to Jesus. Take a moment to consider what you hunger for spiritually. What do you need from Jesus?

Imagine Jesus blesses the loaf of bread, tears it in half, and all of a sudden, there are two freshly baked loaves of the most delicious bread in his hands. He hands one to you.

What does this loaf represent? What is something you've been longing for from Jesus? Take some time to let a word or image come to mind. When you know what that loaf is, take a bite of it in your mind's eye.

Then, Jesus hands you the second loaf. It's still fresh and warm. Before tasting this one, what might it represent? What's another thing you need from Jesus? Take a moment to receive a word or image. When you're ready to receive that, imagine yourself taking a bite of the second loaf.

> Oh, taste and see that the LORD is good;
> Blessed is the one who takes refuge in him. (Psalm 34:8)

Take some time to thank Jesus for these fresh loaves of bread. Pray a blessing over this new nourishment, that it would produce beautiful things in your life. Amen.

If you tried that listening prayer activity, well done! I hope you feel nourished in a way only Jesus can provide. I pray that we would continue practicing the faith to give up our meager loaves for the multiplicative provision of Jesus over our lives. Even if it feels like death, in the kingdom of God, there's always resurrection on the other side of death!

7

LETTING GO

It was the anniversary of Rachel's husband's death. He had been gone for six years now. She still missed waking up to the sound of him singing while he prepared breakfast. Matthias was her best friend. They had been through so much together. Rachel supported him when he wanted to start his own business. They lost their daughter in a terrible accident when she was only twelve. They took care of Rachel's elderly parents together. It had been a full life.

She had never had sons, though. No one to carry on the family name or take care of their dear mother in her old age. She had been working as a seamstress for two years after her husband's inheritance ran out. They had never had very much, always just enough.

Last week, Rachel was fired from her job. Her fingers weren't as nimble anymore. She wasn't as fast as her boss wanted her to be. Her eyes were starting to fail her.

"What would Matthias think?" She wondered, as she realized that all she had left were two copper coins in her little coin purse. It was enough for one last meal. Without much thought, Rachel walked out her front door and started wandering through Jerusalem. She just needed to get away. She was lost in a trance, deeply saddened by the state of her life. She was alone and had nothing to her name.

As she walked, she remembered so many of her memories with Matthias. The time he was trying to make her laugh and ended up knocking over a pyramid of pomegranates in the marketplace. Those days when he taught their daughter Sharon about textiles—his business. Their evening walks together at dusk to get fresh bread for supper. All the family trips to the temple.

"The temple," Rachel thought to herself, as she started walking in that direction. "Matthias's favorite place."

After all they had been through, Matthias's faith in God was steady. It's as if each trial made him closer to God. Rachel both admired this trait in her husband and hated it. She had a little more complicated of a view of God. She didn't understand why he would let her go through so much hardship in life, or why she was alone to go through it all now. She had been faithful to God, but she didn't feel like she was seen by him.

Before long, Rachel found herself in the outer courts of the temple. It had been a couple years since she set foot in that space. Her body felt warm all over—anger, sadness, nostalgia of the good times, remembering how Matthias seemed to come alive at the temple. Rachel always secretly believed that Matthias would have become a rabbi if he had made it farther in his studies.

"Lord, why? Why did you take him away from me? It's been so long, but I'm just as sad and alone as ever. No one seems to care about this poor, old widow. Do you even care?" Rachel prayed in her heart.

Just as she was about to turn around and walk out, Rachel noticed a small crowd of people listening to a rabbi speak.

Something pulled at her curiosity, and she walked over to the back of the crowd. Rachel recognized this rabbi as Yeshua, the one from Nazareth. He had caused quite a stir in the region over the past couple years. He was known for his strong teaching, his diverse group of students who traveled with him, and his miracles. Most rabbis didn't perform miracles. Most rabbis didn't have disciples from career backgrounds—they were usually lifelong students. Rachel couldn't help but think that Matthias would have loved Rabbi Yeshua.

There was some tension in the air; the scribes seemed to be arguing with the rabbi. One asked him to name the Lord's most important commandment.

"The most important is, 'Hear, O Israel: The Lord our God, the Lord is one. And you shall love the Lord your God with all your heart and with all your soul and with all your mind and with all your strength.' The second is this: 'You shall love your neighbor as yourself.' There is no other commandment greater than these."

And the scribe said to Yeshua, "You are right, Teacher. You have truly said that he is one, and there is no other besides him. And to love him with all the heart and with all the understanding and with all the strength, and to love one's neighbor as oneself, is much more than all whole burnt offerings and sacrifices."

Yeshua responded to him, "You are not far from the kingdom of God."

"Could that really be all, Lord?" Rachel prayed in her heart. "To love you with all of me is all you require? And to love others as well? How can this be when I feel as though love is nowhere to be found in my life? Matthias knew your love, Lord. I'm not sure I do. It is very far from me."

Yeshua continued teaching. "Beware of the scribes, who like to walk around in long robes and like greetings in the marketplaces and have the best seats in the synagogues and the places of honor at feasts, who devour widows' houses and for a pretense make long prayers. They will receive the greater condemnation."

Rachel's eyes grew wide. She felt the rabbi's stare through the crowd. It was as if he knew her story. Soon after Matthias died, when Rachel was visiting the temple, a scribe approached Rachel to offer his skills in handling Matthias's assets now that she was widowed. He had claimed to know Matthias and promised to take care of her for a small fee. In her grief, she obliged. But after a few years, the money and the scribe were long gone. She felt embarrassed, confused, angry, and hopeless. She didn't want to run into any of the scribes, so for the past two years, her temple visits had been few and far between.

The Lord had used this special rabbi to speak to her soul. "You do see me, Lord. You know my story. You love me. You will take care of me, even if the world doesn't."

The crowd dispersed after Yeshua's final word. Almost instinctively, Rachel pulled out her coin purse and walked toward the treasury. For the first time since before Matthias's death, she felt hope for her future. "With God, there will be justice," she thought to herself. "God, you are worth all of me. All I have is yours, from today on," Rachel prayed as she dumped her last two coins into her hand and put them in the treasury.

WHO DO YOU BELONG TO?

Rachel's story is an imaginative telling of a widow's life before the events recorded in Mark 12:41-44:

Jesus sat down opposite the place where the offerings were put and watched the crowd putting their money into the temple treasury. Many rich people threw in large amounts. But a poor widow came and put in two very small copper coins, worth only a few cents.

Calling his disciples to him, Jesus said, "Truly I tell you, this poor widow has put more into the treasury than all the others. They all gave out of their wealth; but she, out of her poverty, put in everything—all she had to live on."

This chapter is the basis of our core spiritual invitation during Mark Camp, a yearly spring break trip to Catalina Island. It's a week off the grid, surrounded by the beauty of the Pacific Ocean, deep in the Word together. This might possibly be my favorite thing I do on staff with InterVarsity.

We split the book in half at the very center of Mark, when Peter declares that Jesus is the Messiah. The second half of the book (which we refer to as "Mark Two") consists mainly of Jesus' journey to the cross, and we explore the themes of suffering, death, and resurrection. I've taught Mark Two on five separate occasions. For some reason, I love sitting in the struggle with students. I love being in the midst of the overturning of our idolatry. It's tough and beautiful, like life is.

What is Scripture study without a great application? (Just not as full, in my opinion.) In addition to the widow's story, coins are also mentioned earlier in Mark chapter twelve, when a group of Pharisees and Herodians are trying to trap Jesus. They ask him if he believes in paying the Imperial Tax—a tax for non-Roman citizens that goes to Caesar. Essentially, they ask him, "Where does your loyalty lie?" Jesus was often seen dining with tax collectors, the traitors of their people and friends of Romans. Plus, Jesus makes it very clear that he knows that these religious leaders are not in support of him. They hope to trap him in some sort of religious betrayal.

But like he often does, Jesus responds in the most clever, profound, and prophetic way.

> "Why are you trying to trap me?" he asked. "Bring me a denarius and let me look at it." They brought the coin, and he asked them, "Whose image is this? And whose inscription?"
>
> "Caesar's," they replied.
>
> Then Jesus said to them, "Give back to Caesar what is Caesar's and to God what is God's."
>
> And they were amazed at him. (Mark 12:13-17)

In making sense of this interaction for the students, we note that Jesus not only speaks literally here, but metaphorically as well. Jesus is known for speaking against materialism, and speaking truth to power, but he isn't concerned about Rome. He simply isn't the messiah they were expecting, the one they thought would overthrow Rome and put Israel in charge once again. Instead, he says, "Sure, give Caesar what's his, but give God what's *his*."

And what belongs to God? Where is God's image and inscription stamped?

On us. We are his.

Some of the religious leaders of the day were far from God. Although they made their entire lives about religious loyalty and study of the Law of God, they didn't seem to recognize him standing among them. They wanted rid of Jesus. But Jesus calls them back to what they need.

To them and to us, he says, *Give yourself back to God.*

We let the students sit with this question: What of yourself and your life belongs to God but you're holding on to? To what things do you cling so tightly that Jesus would say, *Let go, release?*

The students carry pennies around in their pockets or place them on their tables to look at during the sessions. What do these pennies represent?

On the night we read the widow's passage, we invite the students to be like her. To consider their pennies, and give them up when they feel ready. Throughout the rest of the week, a student can, at any moment, decide to give up their pennies. They announce it to the group, share what their pennies represent, and then we pray for them.

But, in order to lead a group of students in such an intense application, we must first model it ourselves. I make sure to show up to the session that night ready to throw in my own pennies. And what else do you think my pennies were about that year?

My singleness, duh.

Nearly three years prior, when God blew me away with his sovereignty on the Great Wall and in my life, I had not surrendered myself to his future for me. I just said yes to trusting him more, and that was hard enough. Learning to build that trust can be a delicate process when you're still holding on to what little security you feel you have left. My loneliness and depression had felt like a long, unending road.

The story of Jesus observing the widow's gift is compelling because it raises so many more questions. It invites that imaginative reading of her life. How did Jesus know what those pennies meant to her? Why would she give her last bit of value away? This little moment, days before his death, gives us a glimpse into what Jesus was paying attention to. A single woman and her faith. He saw someone, who couldn't provide for herself, give all that she had left into the offering. What did that mean to her? To give away her sure thing—a sure meal at least! Was her act meant to be between her and the Lord? Was she asking him for something? What was this act of trust?

A single woman who has loved and lost was choosing to trust God *again*.

There are people all over Scripture who, in saying yes to God's call on their lives, bore the burden of never getting to live a normal life or perhaps the life they dreamed up for themselves. And there are those who found themselves in lonely places of unwanted and unplanned singleness. Don't just take my word for it, go find those stories. The widow's is just one of them.

ANOTHER HIKE?

At Mark Camp, I was annoyed with myself *again*. How could I be here *again*? I was still gripping onto pennies—my expectations for what my life should be, and my desire for marriage. This time, I was just annoyed that I hadn't let go yet. I was afraid of what it would mean for my life if I did let go. In my prayer and preparation to model letting go of my pennies for the benefit of my students, God told me to take a hike.

Not just any hike: *the* hike. For years as camp emcee, I had announced that halfway through camp, we would have an extended break time instead of an afternoon session so that people could hike over the island into Avalon if they wanted. But I never went. Didn't even dream of it. I knew it was hard. It's all up, up, up! I knew I'd be left behind if I went on the hike.

So when God told me, *Go on the hike*, I was like, "Nah, no thanks, I'm good."

Go on the hike, Bridget.

That week at camp was foggy and wet every day. The sun hadn't broken through the clouds for a second. There was talk of canceling the hike and I was a little relieved, to be honest. The morning of the hike, it was still gloomy, so I prayed.

"God, if you really want me to go, the sun is going to have to come out. Or else we'll have to cancel it for everyone. If you do that, I'll go."

Sure enough, right before lunch, the sun burst through the clouds and Campus by the Sea came alive. Now I had to go on the hike. So, I made a deal with myself: since I had to take count of the hikers, I would just trail last. I would bring extra water and my inhaler and listen to a playlist the whole time. I would *plan* to be alone. That way I wouldn't feel abandoned.

After counting every hiker, I turned toward the trail and I climbed. It was grueling. It felt like a living metaphor—the effort it takes to keep going when the way is steep, remembering to take breaks and enjoy the scenery sometimes. I prayed that God would give me literal strength at the hard parts of the hike, and I swear he did! On one of my breaks, I took a moment to look out on the Pacific Ocean. It was clear enough to see the mountains in Los Angeles.

"God, before I offer up these pennies tonight, I have one last beef with you."

God is okay with our beef. He can sit in that tension with our anger, frustration, impatience, and confusion. He's even okay not being who we want him to be or giving us what we want him to give us. Now that I think of it, he sounds like the opposite of me! What an amazing example he sets by being present in our conflict with us. He doesn't withdraw when we feel hard things, even if it feels like he does.

"Why do you answer all my prayers except my prayer for a husband? You could be a little more consistent in not answering some of them so that I get used to it. Why is the one thing that I want the most the only thing you won't give me?"

It's true. God had given me everything else. I didn't even ask for his life, but he gave it to me when I was three. I hadn't asked for an extra helping of faith, but here I was, Miss NeverDoubt. Not to mention all the things I *had* asked for—he overdelivered!

In fact, one of the most romantic answers to prayer had happened right there on Catalina Island. When I was twelve years old, I went to science camp at Catalina Island Marine Institute, just one dock over from Campus by the Sea. I had the time of my life that week: climbing the mountain and learning a rain song; getting caught in the middle of my nightly routine when news of a bison broke out on the beach (I ran to see it, toothbrush in hand); snorkeling and hating it; touching sea creatures and loving it. I thought I had found my calling as a marine biologist—that's how alive I felt that week. In my little twelve-year-old heart I said to God, "Can I please come back and work here?" I loved it.

And there I was, standing on a rock in the middle of the ocean, working with students through faith and spirituality rather than in marine biology (God is merciful). He answered even my passing prayers. My flippant temporary longings were realized years later. If you think God doesn't hear you when you pray, just know he listens more closely than you imagine.

No wonder I was so confused and frustrated about why God wouldn't answer my prayer for a husband as timely as the rest.

And then God said something I hadn't heard from him before.

And what if I never do, Bridget? What if this is the one thing I never answer?

So, let's do the same thought experiment that we ask the students to do with their pennies. What if God never gives you the thing you want most?

I'm sure the widow wanted her husband back. I'm sure she wanted a sure thing—a sure meal, a sure future, something to hope for. That's not wrong. Just as I've said before, nothing is wrong with our desire for a spouse and all that comes with marriage.

What if my future isn't what I expect it to be? What if I never get kissed again? What if a man never finds me precious? What if I never know such deep intimacy and love? What if I never get to create a life and family with a partner? What if, year after year, I have to endure this alone? What if I continue to have feelings for men in my life, never to have them returned? What if I always have to keep wondering?

I think in the past, I imagined that the answer to those questions was that my life would be dreadful. I imagined myself turning more cynical, ugly, and stonehearted. I figured I would become prideful and isolate myself from others. Without imagining a future spouse, I felt lost to any kind of vibrant life for myself. That future looked grim to me.

This is why we do this application of Mark Two. We have to identify the things that we think we can't live without: our idols, our wrong beliefs, our bad patterns. We cling so tightly to those pennies, but that's exactly what they are—small change!

The reason God asked me on a hike was because he wanted to remind me of what he said to me on the side of a mountain in China.

Will you trust me, Bridget?

In 2015, I had said a resounding yes, but look what had come of my life! I left China, headed to Tucson, only to walk into a season of depression, in which I so lacked trust in the ways he would come after me and love me. Even though I had said yes with my mouth, with my life I said, "Maybe not?"

How was I any different from these religious leaders? Pledging my life to ministry and The Way of God and yet living like I was running on empty. My soul was crushed, my eyes blind, my heart broken. I knew God was for me, but did I let him be?

In so many ways, I couldn't stop him.

But in other ways, I hadn't let him. I hadn't asked him how I should make money, or develop community, or take chances on relationships or new experiences. I kept doing things my way. Not choosing vulnerability but hiding from everyone how vulnerable I truly was. I was stubborn and angry.

And even though he had begun to shape me into Woman of God Bridget, I hadn't ever really told him that it was okay if I was single for the rest of my life. I had never been willing to say, "It's fine with me, God, if you never answer this prayer." I wasn't okay with that. That didn't feel like an okay option. Because what would it mean if I did?

So, there I was on this beautiful island, the sun shining brightly for the first time in days, alone with God, and he says,

And what if I never answer this prayer?

I thought for a moment and began to cry. Not because I just heard God tell me that I was single for life, but because I realized that when faced with this particular hypothetical, nothing actually changes.

"Then nothing!" I told God.

I wasn't going anywhere. I wasn't abandoning him for the one thing he hasn't done for me.

He's too good.

He's the God who answers the prayers of twelve-year-old Bridget. The God who plucks me out of journal pages and puts me on mountainsides. The God who gives me really great taste in men and healthy relationships after I'm let down by them. He's the God who has protected me from so much pain and confusion. And that's just to name some of the ways he's good to me!

I don't know if this is a quote by a famous theologian, but I heard it from one of the most important theologians in my life: my dad. He has said to me many times, "Bridget, God is pre-dict-ab-ly good!" (always overenunciating the syllables). And he's so right! We can predict every day that God will be good to us.

He's the one with grace for us in our weakness. He's the one who sees us when we are alone. He's listening, paying attention, delighting in us just as we are. He's the romantic one, remember?

Standing there on Catalina Island, I hadn't forgotten his goodness to me, his extravagance. So, I turned around and kept climbing. And I'm not kidding when I say he truly gave me a pep in my step. I caught up with the students, who were laughing, having a good time, and encouraging one another. I practically ran down the road into Avalon and got there just in time to march right onto the boat for the ride back to camp. I wasn't even mad that I didn't get to explore the little tourist town or get an ice cream cone. I was just so happy that I knew I could throw my pennies in that night.

I could finally say to God, "Okay! It's okay if I'm single for the rest of my life! I'll accept it if you want it! My life with you will be predictably good because you are!" I was elated. The sun burst forth on my heart. Freedom and joy were mine once again.

Even though I gave my life to Jesus as a child and continued to pursue God my entire life, I've learned how normal it is to go through cycles like this over and over again, being asked by God to drop our pennies and trust him with our lives and all the future unknowns.

Little Kid Bridget was cool and all, but Grown-Up Me has needed these moments with God to peel off the layers of things holding me back from becoming a more whole and real version of myself. All my yeses to him were followed up with mercy, grace, and steadfast love. Even though he never told me whether I will be single for life or not, he wasn't teasing me. He wasn't withholding any goodness from me; I promise you that! He was freeing me from the things that weighed me down. The parts of me that kept me from growing.

I'll follow the example of Mark and won't finish my imaginative telling of Rachel's story. We have no idea what happens to the widow after Jesus points her out to his disciples. We know, however, that she is seen and cherished. I have a hard time believing they let her get very far without inviting her to join them. In our holy imaginations, we get to trust that the dropping of pennies is hardly the end of the story. It's usually a new beginning.

HERE I AM, LORD

Later that summer, I tasted new beginnings during our global program in Mexico. That was the best summer of my life by far. I started to feel like myself again in this lovely, romantic, mountainous region of Mexico.

I had a gorgeous moment during one of our fiestas. Standing on the balcony while it rained, looking out over the lights of the city, enjoying the cool breeze, I found myself content, reflecting on the trip. I was so happy to be there, surrounded by people, laughter, celebration, and delicious food. We were in a colonial-style city that buried its powerlines underground so you could walk through the cobblestone streets and imagine you were in a time before electricity. Life that summer was sublime. Stopping to get a *cafecito* on the way to English class and chatting up the café owners. Running through the streets like such *gringas* during a monsoon, the whole town standing in doorways and under awnings, watching the heavy rain, and then watching us joyfully singing through the streets, soaked from head to toe, being ridiculously American. I got to lead worship in Spanish on my ukulele in a *pueblito* in the desert countryside.

I became this person I never imagined I would get to be. I spoke a different language, I played an instrument, I traveled, I had a career focused on sharing the good news. My life *was* a dream. And I was so glad I didn't have someone back home waiting for me. Because then I'd have been distracted from the beauty of it all. I would have wanted to be in two places. It was one of the most romantic summers of my life. God was wooing me.

The women who run Compa, InterVarsity's Mexican sister movement, inspire me. They defy social norms—getting married much later in life, giving so much of their time to the cause of bringing the kingdom of God to Mexican students, mostly through volunteerism. They felt like family to me that summer. They made sure to let me know that I was a strong woman too, that I was doing something worthwhile. I could be my goofy, romantic self, and yet deeply serious about the

kingdom of God coming to all nations. It was a gift and a reminder I would need again in the future.

I came back from Mexico knowing I wanted more of that. I
wanted to be in the places where I am my best self, to take
students places where we are sure to grow as followers of Jesus,
meeting God in other parts of the world and seeing how he's
the same everywhere. Beholding the ways he does his thing
all over the map.

A couple weeks later, at our regional staff conference, I
asked my supervisors if I could attend another global program
the following summer. And they said yes. It was my plan to go
abroad every summer if I could, while I could. I wanted to take
advantage of my singleness, and I wanted to taste more of the
real Bridget.

Normally, our regional conference is a time of renewal and
revisioning for the upcoming school year, but I was wary of
being the same Bridget I had been before Mexico—tired, saying
yes to things I needed to say no to, not creating work-life
boundaries. During one session that was meant to be inspiring
and exciting, I was on the verge of a panic attack. I began to
hear the same old lies as before.

*You're not enough. Do better. Be better. Give up all your time,
all your life, make things happen.*

I must've looked like a deer in the headlights because my
boss beelined it to me when the session finished.

"How are you doing?" he asked.

"I need a miracle, Steven. I can't keep doing this."

He knew what the last couple years had been like for me
and wanted to see a change in the upcoming year of ministry.
"I know. Meet me before dinner tonight in the lobby, and we're
gonna ask God for a miracle."

I loved his confidence, and I appreciated the care. When we met in the lobby that night, we dove right into classic Inter-Varsity prayer ministry.

Steven and I started to listen for the Holy Spirit, and he quickly had this sense of all my anxiety and depression being sucked right out of me. When he told me that, I actually felt a whooshing sensation from my body. I was curious and surprised, so I let him know. Steven had just returned from his sabbatical and felt inspired to help me pray a simple prayer, like something he would pray in his times spent listening for God's voice.

Steven had me repeat, "Here I am, Lord, suck it out," multiple times.

I know. So weird.

But honestly, God is weird. Every time I repeated that phrase, I could feel a burden lift and my load get lighter. By the end of our prayer time, Steven blessed me, and suddenly I felt new. I remember telling him, "I hope this lasts."

The next morning, I woke up with a song on my heart, bursting out of my soul. She was back. Woman of God Bridget, a skip in her step! I was freed. Healed. And I couldn't believe it.

God was merciful to melt my depression away. My renewed strength sent me forward into the following year to make better choices for my life as Woman of God Bridget, a Bridget made new.

Now, I don't want to make light of anyone's depression by sharing the story of how quickly mine left. That really was a miracle for me. Depression can be debilitating. Loneliness like that can feel so isolating and dark. If you're still in a season of depression, I want you to know that I see you and that there is hope for you, even if you don't know when or how relief will come.

Jesus saw the widow in the temple and he knew the rest of her story. He honored her. Every day I hope I can channel her bravery and how she took a wild chance on the God she knew loved her.

He sees us too. He knows our stories and our futures. Don't shortchange yourself. Make the best trade of all by giving yourself back to God. And this must happen repeatedly. Daily. Monthly. Annually. Would you bet your life on what Jesus has for you like the widow did? He's a winning bet, every time. Jesus bet his life so that you could! Take him up on the offer of eternal resurrection life. That's two cents worth giving!

Pilgrimage Moment: Holy Imagination

Does it ever occur to you that imagination is a holy and miraculous thing? In my mind's eye, I can imagine any number of animals, colors, and worlds. I can create pictures and new ideas in my head! If you think about it too long, it might start to blow your mind too. This is because our imaginations are holy. God gave us the ability to imagine something different from the realities before us. While so often we use this skill to escape those realities, God intends that we use it to live into new ones.

In order to live into the resurrection life we're offered, we need to be able to imagine different futures for ourselves. As single people, we need to let our imaginations run wild for all types of lives we could be living. I've said this from the beginning of the book, but the current cultural context for Christian singleness is unimaginative. We can change that.

Holy imagination is a hard practice. As Curt Thompson puts it, in order to make some movement in our imaginations for ourselves, we need confessional community who can help us create a vision for ourselves. On pilgrimage, you don't usually know what's on the path ahead.

To co-labor with Christ (1 Corinthians 3:9) to bring new creation, new elements of beauty and goodness, into being requires an expansion of our imaginations—one that entails great effort. . . . Before we live into a different future, we must imagine it, and for us to imagine our future as God does, we will need help in particular, for no human is going to imagine the future as God does.[1]

You haven't been there or experienced it yet. However, your fellow pilgrims can help you reimagine what could be coming up. Readjust your view of your future. This pilgrimage moment is a little more conceptual in that I hope my story so far is helping you reimagine what your life can look like as a single person. Not as a mirror to mine, but as an expanded view for what God might have for you on the other side of giving yourself more fully to him.

Before you move on, call up a friend or talk to your roommate about what's been happening in you so far. Share with them about your loaves of bread, your pennies, or what's holding you back from being able to engage with those symbols. They may be able to help you move forward into a holier imagination for your life.

8

EMBRACING MY AUTHENTIC SELF

I could tell I was getting on my team leader's nerves.

It was my second trip to China, three years after my first visit, and I was serving on a team with two other InterVarsity staff members: Erin, who was directing the trip, and Kaleb. Before the trip, one of our regional leaders called to ask how I thought I would get along with Erin. She is younger than me, so I think they were anticipating tension there. Age wasn't an issue for me—it's my job to champion college students in their authority and giftings, and it would be silly not to do the same for Erin. However, I could still sense that there might be conflict, I just wasn't sure what it would be. It turned out that me being myself was the culprit.

In case this hasn't already come across, I am my best self on our global programs. I can adapt, cross cultures, think on my feet, lighten the overall mood of the team, have serious conversations, and have silly experiences, just to name a few things. This is a part of my job where I fire on all cylinders. But on this particular trip, my best self was not completely accepted outright. God used my teammates to help refine my sense of who I am made to be.

An unexpected feature of our trip turned out to be the Enneagram. Kaleb was digging into it by reading through *The Road Back to You*,[1] so Erin and I decided to join him. The Enneagram is a personality type indication tool that helps you learn about how you developed and what your core motivations and longings are. There are nine types that you can identify with as your core; typically you relate more to one or the other of the wings on either side of your number. All the types are interconnected, so it doesn't box you in completely. It has become popular in Christian culture over the last few years, helping us face deeper realities about the cycles and habits we find ourselves stuck in. It also provides clear vision for health and paths to get there. I had known that I wasn't totally set on my number, but I didn't care to face the truth until they convinced me to read along.

I'm really grateful that reading this book with Kaleb went hand in hand with my conflict with Erin. Without one or the other, I'm not sure I would have grown so much that summer.

HOLY MISBEHAVIOR

One Saturday, we went to see the Terracotta Warriors, an ancient site where a former emperor of China had set up an army of clay figures. It was a tourism day with the students. We were hot, it was crowded, but we were seeing ancient history, not something we encounter much in the United States. By the time we were leaving for an afternoon meal, I could tell everyone was worn out. With us were some Chinese students and the Chinese professor who was the liaison to the program for the university. We split into two round tables at lunch.

I *excel* at group meals. We have something to focus on together, we can ask questions, and our mood improves with every bite! At my table, we were having a great time laughing and getting to know each other, and I was encouraging the American students to try some of the foods they were afraid of. At one point, we were all chanting a Chinese cheer for one student to eat the eyeball of the sweet-and-sour fish laid out before us. (FYI: It tastes like fish, so it turns out it's not that big of a deal after all.)

At the other table though, they were having the opposite experience. They seemed tired and bored, and even though they were feet away, I could tell that Erin's mood was not happy. I wasn't sure why, and I didn't want to read into it, but I did get up to see if I could work a little of my magic on their table as well. I had very little luck. At that point, I sensed Erin was mad at me, but I couldn't understand why. I watched as she and Kaleb went off to talk about it. He's such a peacemaker (Enneagram Nine), so I knew he was trying to help her understand me.

The truth is, I was being fully myself. I was offering the best of me in that scenario and yet it was unappreciated by my coworker. I could feel that even without being told. Later on, Kaleb admitted to me that Erin was stressed out because of my rambunctious behavior. He didn't shame me though. He didn't even discourage me from being myself. He just let me know how Erin was feeling.

Eventually, Erin tried to address it in a roundabout way by making up a hypothetical about a student and asking for my advice about what to do. I think it backfired because I responded that sometimes, people are going to be who they are, and you have to let them. At the time I had no clue she was talking about me. So when we finally talked it out and she admitted that, I was amused.

Unfortunately, friends have asked me to not be myself many times. I wish I could say otherwise, but sometimes they feel embarrassed by my directness and big personality. This was one of the first times in a long time that being myself felt costly, and I didn't want to budge. Normally, I would have already anticipated Erin's needs and desires in that situation. She was embarrassed by my fun-loving behavior because of how direct and loud and energetic I am compared to typical Chinese behavior, which we perceive as quiet and meek, and tends to be indirect. She saw my ways of relating and connecting as disrespectful because they were starkly different from the Chinese way.

I apologized for stressing Erin out, and for making her feel embarrassed, but I wouldn't apologize for my personality. I can't confirm this, but our Chinese friends did not seem offended or embarrassed by my behavior. I felt very encouraged by them to be myself, which was a breath of fresh air.

What Erin expected of me though, made sense for her. At the time she was realizing that she's a One on the Enneagram. Ones see the world in their own way; there is a particular set of right and wrong in their eyes, and it's based off what they've observed in their lives. Erin was trying to be a good director and didn't want the American teachers to offend or break trust with the Chinese teachers. She was afraid that I was doing that during the times I was having fun and being silly with the students. Because Ones are the resident rule-followers, they also want people to know that they too are capable of fun. They just want to be seen as good and right. Rule following and fun are both good and right things.

It seemed though, that the cultural value of saving face was more important to her than my way of interacting with the students. She thought I was doing the opposite when I was goofing off with them. I think that she just didn't feel like I was saving *her* face.

When she finally came out with her true feelings toward me, I was a mixed of relieved and shocked. So often, I can read people far off, far before they show their cards to me. That's a common trait of a Two, the Enneagram number I began to realize best described me. Twos spend our entire developmental years assessing our situations for how to best be loved and valued. We pick up on the cues people give when they aren't happy—when they aren't getting what they want and need. This becomes a useful trait in many ways. We have eyes to see when we should give up our seat on the bus or at a party. We foresee when people will need things and prepare for it. We are tremendous hosts and incredibly thoughtful and considerate. These traits of mine were at work in China.

It's a wonder that, when I heard that Erin was mortified by my behavior, I didn't cower and apologize and proceed to behave in the fashion she wanted me to. For some reason I wasn't concerned about protecting her feelings at the expense of being myself.

That summer the Holy Spirit was mercifully releasing me from the patterns that led me to be depressed and unhealthy. In China, I felt so much freedom in my relationships with our Chinese friends—I felt like Woman of God Bridget—but I was being told that my way of relating was unacceptable. And I disagreed. This wasn't my first trip to China, nor was it my first time crossing cultures.

Using the Enneagram helped me see how the person I am can be a gift, and how to address my hang-ups in order to step toward health. So, I pushed back at Erin's claims. And I realized that this was where our conflict would be: Would she be able to love me on this trip? Would I be loved and taken care of by my director?

It was the same question I had asked in any given situation. I was seeking to please people (another common character-istic of Enneagram Twos) in hopes of feeling loved.

Instead of turning from Erin and putting up walls be-cause I didn't think she could love me well, and instead of bending to her desires, I engaged in the conflict of it. I didn't worry what the outcome would be. I let go of control. I was going to be comfortable with her disapproval because I dis-agreed with it. I told her that I needed her to love me well. I needed her to give me grace, trust me with the students, both Chinese and American. I needed her to see me as Woman of God Bridget, not Bridget Who Will Ruin Reputa-tions. I don't think I am even close to being capable of that kind of destruction.

In the past, I might have followed Erin's example in acting more mature and professional in the sight of the students and university officials. But this was a weird new invitation from God.

Don't worry about behaving.

Wow, what an invite! For me, this means not apologizing for being myself.

It means actually telling people when they hurt or disap-pointed me.

It means asking for what I wanted and needed, even when it feels like death.

It means being really goofy sometimes, even if it makes other people cringe.

It means taking time for myself, dreaming my own dreams.

Even though God had been gently inviting me into all of this for my entire adulthood, something clicked for me that summer in China. The invitation felt so new to me, and really scary. I was shocked to realize how much of my life I had been "behaving" just to be loved.

I AM NOT A PHONY

One day, I had taught a lesson to our class and released the partners to have conversations for the rest of our time together. Meanwhile, I was reading back through my journal to see if there was proof of my people-pleasing tendencies all along. Realizing that I'd been functioning this way for so long was such a gut punch for me. My coworker Kaleb came and sat with me while the students were chatting away with their partners.

"What are you doing?" he asked. Clearly, he was bored of his own journaling and wanted some extrovert time.

"Well, if you must know, I was reading back through my journal," I said.

"Why?" he asked.

"To find evidence of my patterns. Realizing I'm a Two on the Enneagram has really messed me up."

"What do you mean?"

"I feel like such a sham," I admitted.

"Why?"

"Because nothing I do is the real me. I just do things I think people want me to do. I choose things I think people want me to choose. I act and say things that will get me loved. I'm a joke. No one actually knows the real me. I'm not sure I even do."

Kaleb laughed kindly and let out a sigh. "Okay, Bridget. First of all, I get why you feel that way, but do you really think that's true?"

"Yes. You don't know me. I've tricked you," I said. I was feeling bratty.

"Oh really, okay. So you're saying that when you're having important conversations with the students, that's not the real you?" he challenged.

"Well . . . okay fine, that's the real me."

"And when you're galloping like a horse on your way to the dining hall just to make Michelle laugh, that's not the real you?" He smiled playfully.

"Ugh, okay, fine. That's the real me too. But I did cause that bike cop to crash because I was being a distraction. The real me is dangerous," I shot back.

"Sure, she is! Either way, you may be right that some of the time, you are not being your true self. But we see you, Bridget. We see the real you in all your silliness and all your seriousness. The real you is a gift to us. You're not a phony." Kaleb preached to my soul.

I needed to hear that. I needed to know that people see me, even when I don't have eyes to see myself. Yet again, God was using a summer abroad to peel back another tentacle of my Octopus of Brokenness. I needed to fully embrace myself for all the good and all the bad. I needed to be able to see my authentic self and choose to be her, no matter the cost, because the reward would be freedom.

GETTING LOVED ANYWAY

My interaction with Erin that summer served to expose and rid me of this need to please others at the expense of my authentic self. My interaction with Kaleb served to speak truth and call me into the invitation of holy misbehavior. The best people in my life have been the ones who have given me permission to break societal rules in order to experience freedom. That's some of the most prophetic kingdom of God stuff you can do for people: call them into who God created them to be and out of who the world is asking them to be. Kaleb and Erin partnered with God in the journey he prepared for me that summer, whether they knew it or not.

In fact, at our final banquet, I managed to strike up a little more conflict with Erin because she was worried again that I was being disrespectful when I was being playful with the students. I was mad that at the first moment I tried to be myself and misbehave a little, she was right there trying to get me to sit down. I knew we'd have to talk it out later that night.

After the banquet, we were out on the sports fields with our students and Chinese friends, hugging, taking pictures, and exchanging gifts as is customary at the end of these programs. Several of the girls wrote on postcards to let me know that they felt inspired by my joy to let loose and be a little braver. They said that they hoped they could be more like me in the future. What an honor. I felt so humbled that they seemed to see me for my truest self and said that it was a gift to them.

As I walked back to our room that night, I asked the Holy Spirit to fill me up and help me reconcile with Erin. I needed to share my true feelings, no matter the outcome. I didn't know if Erin would see me or love me in it. I guessed she would stand her ground that she was not wrong for wanting me to behave a certain way, but I had to tell her that it hurt me.

As we sat on our beds across the room from each other, I felt complete peace in contrast with the frustration I could see emanating from Erin.

"Erin, you know how I'm a Two on the Enneagram?" I started.

"Yes . . ." she replied.

"Well, earlier today I was having an existential crisis be-cause of it. I've been feeling like I've made all my decisions based off everyone else's desires or what they want for me. Most of my life I've behaved in the way that I knew would get me loved, rather than out of my authentic self. I came into the banquet feeling zapped—like a total fraud. It's something I've been struggling with this summer."

"Okay . . ." she answered, unsure where I was going with this.

"So when you stopped me from engaging with the students, I was mad. I wanted to laugh and be a little silly, to get my mind off my problems. But the first moment I was trying to be myself today, you were right there trying to correct my be-havior. So, I sat down. And I'm sorry for my reaction. I was not gracious. I just also wanted you to know where I was coming from. It has hurt my feelings this summer when you haven't trusted my interactions with the students. In those moments, it feels like you don't appreciate me for who I am."

Erin had a quizzical look on her face, "But Bridget, you were acting ridiculous. You wanted to sing a song with the students about mooning the sun!"

Yes, I did.

That summer, I had taught our American students a song I made up with a Disney princess–like melody and one line that repeats, "Have you ever mooned the sun?" over and over. It was a goofy, catchy tune that we couldn't get out of our heads. Well, our students taught their Chinese peers, and that's what they were doing at the banquet when someone suggested we record it, and Erin quickly shot the idea down.

"Yeah, I did! And I don't see a problem with that. They're college students," I replied to Erin's accusation.

"I can't believe you think that's okay!" Erin exclaimed. See, she wasn't as worried about the song as she was about communicating to our Chinese counterparts that we were disrespectful and didn't want to save face for them or with them.

"Erin, I understand why you don't think it's okay, but I don't think it would have caused as much harm as you're worried it would. You can be wrong and right at the same time in different ways. It's good that you want to keep trust; it's just often been at my expense."

Erin looked exasperated. "I feel like you're just trying to get me to apologize to you!"

I paused and took a breath. She was really standing her ground. But for some reason, I didn't feel too worried. I stood up for myself with wisdom and gusto.

"I mean, I mainly wanted to explain to you how I was feeling, and why I behaved the way I did. I would love an apology, but I don't expect one. But I do want you to hear one from me again. I'm sorry for my behavior when you asked me not to have the students record the song. I was curt with you. I was bratty. You don't deserve that."

And that's when it clicked for her. Her countenance changed. After a bit, her voice softened too.

"Bridget, I think that I don't want to be seen as the wet blanket," Erin said. "I've been on these trips before where the other staff were the 'fun staff,' and I wasn't seen that way, even though I really wanted to be. So as the director, I have this huge responsibility of making sure we have good relationships with our Chinese partners, but also this deep desire to be seen as a fun staff by our students."

"You are so much fun, Erin," I chimed in. (She really is super fun, by the way.)

"Thanks. I haven't felt like it. I felt like I had to choose one value over the other. And so, when I saw you having the fun that I wanted to be having, I had dissonance about it. It stressed me out. I'm sorry about how I've treated you because of that."

"I totally forgive you, Erin." I was so proud of the work the Holy Spirit was doing in that room.

We weren't really fighting about a song about mooning the sun. We were both having our own identity crises that summer. My journey intertwined with Erin's. She was learning that she could let loose and have some fun, even when she is in charge. She was learning that what she thinks is right isn't always right. I was learning that I could take the risk to be myself, even if I couldn't guarantee that I would be loved for it, that a little holy misbehavior would bring more freedom than behaving as I was expected to.

Together, we began to let go of our core desires and learn to become the people we were meant to be. It's a trap to think we need to spend our lives trying to prove that we are good, right, lovable, and valuable. It's a trap to spend our lives solely striving for relational stability, personal peace, independence, or individualism. These things aren't always guaranteed or good answers to our deep longings.

What a difference those few hours made. God used both the students and this situation with Erin to free us both. I'm really grateful for that summer with Erin. She was an amazing director. It's a lot of pressure to be the sole director of a global program. And she did a wonderful job, especially having a staff person like me who stressed her out. She demonstrated love for me that summer. I thank God that he opened my eyes to see it, and I'm so grateful for the ways she engaged with my brokenness, forgave me in conflict, and had eyes to see me and a heart to understand me. What a beautiful picture of God's grace and mercy.

Ministry has been one of God's great mercies on me. It's a place where I've seen him call me in. He's given me the strength to stand for what's right, to ask him to do it all, and for me to be filled with the Holy Spirit. I've continued to stay even when I don't get loved because it isn't about me getting loved! It's just about loving others.

The fun part is that you get loved anyway!

RETURNING TO THE GREAT WALL

It was just the right time for me to return to the Great Wall, the scene of my last big fight with God. My last big fit.

The Great Wall has become a sacred place for me. The second time I climbed it, my team knew my story from the first time. A few of my teammates stuck around to climb together, and we had a great time. I was also in better shape than I had been three years prior, so it didn't take me nearly as long as before. It's almost as if God made it harder for me the first time.

So much can change in three years! God had been faithful to show me that even when I don't get everything I want, he still has it all for me. So often, when I prayed prayers for a husband, God showed me that he had far more for me than that. Below the surface of our conflicts and desires are deeper longings, ones I believe only God can address. I wanted to be loved, but God wanted me to be free, because I was already so loved.

I decided to have a little quiet moment alone with God on the Great Wall. I pulled out my journal and thanked God for the amazing life he had given me. I was so happy to be there. I wasn't that concerned about not having a husband, as I had been three years prior. I didn't feel lonely. I knew nothing was wrong with me still being single. I had begun to believe that my truest self was a gift, whether I got the love I wanted or not. I was exactly where I was supposed to be: in the middle of God's grace.

It was only God's work in my life that changed me over those years. It was God who had done great and wonderful things in and through me. All of it was his grace. And my arms were wide open to it. By this time, I knew grace well, and I just wanted more of it.

I don't see my singleness the same way I did that first time on the wall. It doesn't feel like an excruciating climb. It feels a lot more level. There's no final summit with singleness, no ultimate win. Life is a mix of messy and miraculous. Being single gives you this great opportunity to recognize who you really are, undistracted, warts and all. When you do that good and hard work of being a human, all your relationships will benefit. You don't have to use the Enneagram to do it, but the content of the Enneagram helped me look at myself and my friends in a new light.

Pilgrimage Moment: Take a Hike

I've had many moments alone with God on mountainsides and mountaintops. Some of them were intentional on my part and some of them were not. No matter, it was in these spaces that I was able to see myself for who I really am: God's. I was privileged to return to the Great Wall and rewrite that experience, so to speak—to have a living metaphor for God's provision and grace in my life.

You can have these moments too. You've gotta go be alone with your Creator. You've gotta remember who the Divine is, who you are, and renew your covenant together. And it has to happen regularly, because the problems of life will always be waiting at home for you.

Do it in your own creative ways. Do you need to go on a trip you never would otherwise? Do you need to take your sabbath seriously and get unplugged for the day? Do you need to return to a place and let God rewrite its meaning, to show himself to you more clearly? What are some mountainsides you can visit in the near future to steal away for a moment with God? A hike or a walk are simple choices to make.

Even though so many of my mountainside moments with God have been while on the job—activities for fun and tourism with students—God claimed them as spiritual moments between us. You may need to hear different things about your singleness in your alone places with God. If you don't make intentional space to hear from him, God may force you up on mountainsides by his mercy anyway.

9

HOLY ALONENESS

I didn't say yes the first time my pastor and friend Nick invited me to go on the Camino de Santiago. I wanted to go, but it felt crazy to travel across the world to go on a five-hundred-mile hike in Spain, for no other reason than to just do it. Most of my global travels had been attached to work trips, and it felt selfish to go on that big of a trip or spend that much money on just *me*.

A few years later, as Nick was preparing to go again, there was a stronger tug on my heart to go. I was about year away from my six-month sabbatical with InterVarsity. I was still flirting with burnout. I was exhausted and didn't want to get to the end of 2019 stumbling over the finish line. I wanted to enter my sabbatical full of life and hope, and ready to take it on full force. So, in January 2019, I said yes to go on the Camino in May.

In the five months leading up to my trip to Spain, I prayed and trained for the trip. I knew it was something I needed—a separate thing to focus on outside my work life: walking. Walks became so life-giving for me. In my prayers, my expectation for my trip on the Camino was that God would show up in a big way, that he would speak to me and give me a huge revelation, maybe even change my plans. I expected clarity about my job and my future by the time I made it to Santiago de Compostela.

At home, I was restless in my job. I didn't feel like I was good at it. I felt like success stories were not found at my doorstep. And yet, I knew I was called to ministry. So why did I feel like a failure at ministry? Ministry had taught me so much as a single person. And any time I told someone what I did for a living, they would say, "Wow, that must be so rewarding." Rewarding isn't the word I'd use to describe it; it was challenging. There's this weird thing we do with ministry, though. We overromanticize it and maybe even overspiritualize it. We act like it's some magical space or higher calling when it's actually just the stuff of life.

I knew I was called to ministry in high school because I love people. I love having tough conversations. I love loving my friends. I am not interested in much else. But making your whole career about loving people? It's not cute. It's rough. It's a choice to die to yourself daily and then when you try and find life elsewhere, to die again! Ministry is not mainly success stories. It's real life. It's relationships with people who need love, who need vision, and who need champions, people in their corner. Ministry is just a chance to bring the kingdom of God near to others. And often, it's very unexciting.

Outsiders of Jesus' ministry were typically judgmental of his approach. They were confused and grossed out that he would spend time with sinners, lepers, and others considered unclean. And yet, people surrounded Jesus constantly. They craved his healing, his words, his teaching, his presence. They were constantly trying to take from Jesus, and yet he continued to give compassion.

"Very early in the morning, while it was still dark, Jesus got up, left the house and went off to a solitary place, where he prayed" (Mark 1:35).

Jesus would regularly steal away from it all. He would go and clear his head, because I'm sure he was overwhelmed with human emotion and recognized his human capacity. He knew the essential nature of being alone. So, he'd go on a hike. I wonder if he asked no one to follow him, or if the disciples just didn't like hiking. Or did they know that it was Jesus' alone time and they respected it? I don't know. I do know that Jesus was intentional about being alone. I like to imagine him sitting on the side of a hill, eating a fish sandwich after feeding a mass of people, decompressing because of his frustration at the disciples' lack of faith and compassion after everything they had seen: *Will this really work? Will they really listen? Will they really be the ones to bring my good news to the world? God, they are so* human. *And I'm human here, right now, too. And it's frustrating.*

That is what my Camino was about: my humanity.

I was so hesitant to go on a trip that would expose my humanity, that would feed it, tend to it, slow down my you're-only-good-for-producing attitudes. How would three weeks away be productive? How would a trip just for me benefit others?

But when did my every waking hour become about benefiting all of humanity? I was doing this very normal human ministry for years, thinking I was supposed to be saving the world. Jesus is the only human in history to have saved the world. Why did I think I was an exception?

I needed to steal away like he had. So, he gave me the gift of a Camino.

FACING MY OWN HUMANITY

My first day on the Camino, after two days of travel, I was dropped off by a minibus in the middle of the countryside in north-central Spain. I had found the most affordable option to get me where I needed to go to meet my friends, and there wasn't even a stop in that town! Luckily, the Spanish locals have mercy on pilgrims. So, they made up a bus stop for me, pushed me out the door, told me to just keep walking, follow the yellow arrows, and I would make it to the tiny town of Mansilla de las Mulas up ahead. My friends would arrive the next day.

Once there, I had to find a place to rest that night. Talk about channeling Joseph and Mary as they entered Bethlehem . . . will there be room for me? There was. I had jet lag and a cold at the time, so I slept the afternoon away in the dorm room full of bunks. As other pilgrims came in and out of the room, I heard them ask about me, because they hadn't seen me before. I woke up and told them who I was, why I was appearing out of nowhere, alone, in the middle of the Camino. All in Spanish. And then I asked about where I should go for dinner to have my first pilgrim meal alone.

It's a weird loneliness to be in a place across the world where everyone speaks different languages, and me only speaking a moderate amount of the local language, just enough to get by. Waiting for my friends to join me, I felt so out of place. My aloneness was palpable. All I wanted to do was sleep and wake up the next morning with my friends in town, but I would have to wait an entire Sunday morning before their arrival.

As the sweet *hospitaleros* ushered me out of the pilgrim hostel, or *albergue*, that morning, they were kind enough to give me some cough drops and crackers and send me on my way. I tried my best not to cry in front of them, but as I walked away from the building, the tears came. I went and sat on a bench in a square, and I wept.

I felt like an imposter in Mansilla. It was 8:15 a.m., and the bench I chose faced a giant statue of pilgrims at the foot of a cross, as if they had thrown themselves there at the end of a day's tired journey. I let myself cry, and I let myself be curious about why I felt so unnerved.

Nowhere to go, nothing to do, no responsibilities, no distractions or people. What do we do? Being truly alone is scary. We aren't comfortable with it.

I think this is why some of us hate being single. Being alone is uncomfortable. We would prefer the distraction and attention of others to help us interact with the world.

At that moment, I was feeling the limitations of my humanity. I was feeling the tension of being in the in-between, the waiting place. I've thrived off of my external circumstances, the people in my life, the things I produce. The walk on the Camino was an invitation into my own humanity and my frustration with it.

In White American culture, we treat time as such a commodity. Time should produce something. It should make goods or money or value. The early bird gets the worm. We're supposed to turn time into something other than time. If we don't, we shame ourselves. We've "wasted" our time. White American society uplifts this hustle culture, but it's inhumane.

As I sat there contemplating my next moves, God sent a Saint Bernard to love on me. It was a giant dog, fluffy and friendly. As its owner came up to join it, we shared some Spanish small talk, and my spirits felt revived. I could tell the owner was used to his dog stealing the show. I'm sure that dog had met many pilgrims in all different states of mind, and honestly, he snapped me out of my sadness. Even though I was alone without any friends, it didn't take long for me to encounter some kindness and affection. I hadn't even moved from my bench.

I kind of knew that the next couple weeks were going to look like the stony pilgrims before me—having a holy moment alone at the foot of the cross.

WHOLLY ALONENESS

Alone is the most sacred place to be.

We see this all over life. When you're conceived, there's a time where only God knows you exist. When you die, no one goes with you. It's just you and God at the beginning and the end of your existence.

We also see all over Scripture that solitude is sacred. God beckons so many of his people out into desert places to speak to them. Or he finds them hidden and isolated and makes himself known. Hagar at the spring (Genesis 16). Jacob alone in the night, wrestling with God (Genesis 32:22-32). Moses and the burning bush (Exodus 3). Elijah in the cave (1 Kings 19:1-9). Jonah watching Nineveh from afar (Jonah 4).

"In the beginning was the Word, and the Word was with God, and the Word was God. He was with God in the beginning. Through him all things were made; without him nothing was made that has been made" (John 1:1-3).

When we are alone with God, we are whole. We are complete because without him nothing was made that has been made. Without him, nothing. Through him, all things.

We need to be alone with Jesus, the Word, to let him speak into our hearts. We need to get away from all the other voices. All other agendas and narratives. The only one that matters is the one that will call us into the light and into his love.

Alone with God is where you can be healed.

It's where you are called.

It's where you are seen and given strength to return to the crowd.

If we never go off alone, things will get murky. We will begin to confuse the voices of others for the voice of God. We will begin to build a life around them, not on a firm foundation.

True solitude is uncomfortable. I don't mean being alone in your bed on a Friday night watching TikToks until 1 a.m. I mean alone, no distractions, paying attention to your body and mind and heart. Sometimes being alone is really about sifting through the real and difficult stuff before you get to deeper issues.

For me, the Camino was so humbling. I did not have all this mental energy to hear God speaking huge revelations about my life like I thought I would. Instead, I was constantly present in my aching body, which every day was over it after six miles. This meant that every morning, a couple hours into the hike, I had to fight against my will and my mind to go another seven to twelve miles. Hiking long distances brings you into your body and at one with your needs.

Honestly, I tried to make this trip to Spain into something super productive. I had these expectations that the Camino would be more than just me walking almost two hundred miles in eleven days across a country I'd never been to.

I was trying to accomplish more than that?!

I genuinely thought I would read and journal every day. Nope. I had no mental space for it. No desire. I just wanted to sit around when I got to my daily destination. I wanted to eat and enjoy the people and the weather.

I didn't anticipate that the Camino would give me a break from a life that was constantly outwardly focused on others' needs and on what I was producing outside of myself. For those two weeks, I focused on me. My body. I know that for a single woman, you'd think I'd have a lot more "me" time, but that's not the way I had set up my life. It wasn't the way I approached my time. It was so nice to take a brain break for a couple weeks. It was wonderful to put everything at home on pause and just focus on putting one step in front of the other. A day or two in, I gave up on paying attention to big life revelations.

The Camino slows you down. The only reason you'd want to be early to your destination is so you have a bed to sleep in that night. You have to stop to get water, to eat lunch, to dry out your feet, to use the bathroom. You can only go as fast as your legs and stamina will carry you. And sometimes there are pretty places to linger.

Every day was a lesson in my own capacity, a new chance to see how far my body would go and what new sights I would see.

It was always midday when I lost my friends Nick and Roshelle because I was no match for their pace on the trail. I'd learned to not let it bother me too much. One particular day after lunch, I took one of my afternoon breaks and got a Coke with lemon and sat outside a restaurant airing out my sweaty feet, so as to not get blisters. I sat in the shade, sipping my drink, watching the occasional pilgrim walk by, nodding and greeting them with the obligatory *buen Camino* benediction. It was quiet, and the weather was beautiful.

And all of a sudden, God was speaking to me.

Bridget, you are exactly where you need to be. You don't need to be one town back or two towns ahead. You need to be here right now, on the Camino, in Spain. You don't need to be at home working and raising money. You don't need to be going on a global program. You don't need to be making money with all your part-time jobs in Tucson. You need to be here, right now, in the cool breeze, in the shade, drinking that Coke with lemon. I gave you the legs you have. I want those legs for you. I want you here.

At the core of our discomfort in being physically or relationally alone, we long for this affirmation. That we are whole, no matter what we're offering, no matter our limitations. We need to experience the freedom of simply existing, to not produce or strive or hustle for a bit. To be gentle with ourselves and treat ourselves with kindness.

On the other hand, you've seen several times in my story so far when being alone with God can be a crying out, a wrestling, a venting session. God wants both for us. He is the safe place. He is the one who will lift our burdens and give us his. He is the one who will listen, speak, and restore us.

Pilgrimage Moment: Solitude

I had the distinct feeling that after this trip, I would learn how to be more present in my body. It felt like an invitation from the Holy Spirit while I walked and ached.

Pay attention to your body.

What was my body telling me?

Slow down? Stretch? Drink some water? Find a toilet! Take a break? Eat a meal, any meal.

I also needed to listen to my emotions. Why was I cranky? Was that okay? What was bringing my soul alive?

The Camino even reminded me that I do remember who I am. In the busyness of my life, I had been forgetting. I dehumanized myself for the sake of progress and production.

All these things were the fruit of me stealing away for no one else but me. It helped me return to myself, to my humanity, to my body, to my desires, to my identity. God made his grace very basic to me in those moments of holy aloneness: I am exactly who and where he wants me to be. I got a sweet taste of freedom.

We need to be kind to ourselves, to return to our humanity and practice holy aloneness. As much as we need community, we need to be alone with God. The desert fathers and mothers in the early church lived ascetic lives in the wilderness so as to not drown in society. They didn't do it as a pious act, but instead to save themselves and society from forgetting God. They did it to clear the cobwebs and get to the basics of their human souls.[1]

If you can learn to be comfortable being alone with yourself and before God, you will open up a flood of freedom in your life too. You may even find yourself more fulfilled than before. Too often, we let our discomfort with being alone lead to quick fixes and poor coping. Embracing solitude proves to be far more productive than anything else. However, there are so many things that get in the way of our ability to practice holy aloneness in everyday life. So many physical, emotional, and mental distractions. Life isn't the Camino, so we have to learn ways to do this in our lives as they are now.

Here are some suggestions:

- Take up a regular practice of meditative prayer, such as centering prayer. It's clearing the mind and focusing on the presence of God.
- Take up a regular practice of yoga and breath work—anything that requires bodily presence and physical focus.
- Take walks without devices. Let yourself observe the world around you for all it has to offer.
- Spend undistracted time with Jesus, letting him speak to you in listening prayer and through the Word.

- Limit your screen time. Just do it, you won't regret it. Let yourself be uncomfortable.
- Turn off your notifications. Have mercy on yourself. You don't have to be at everyone's beck and call; you don't belong to them.
- Do what makes sense for your life and what you are capable of. Start small.

I like to call solitude "holy aloneness" because there are so many versions of unholy aloneness. This is something we have control over. We can choose to make our aloneness holy. We can invite God into it. We can ask him to redeem it. And he will! Even more than we know.

I dare you to find out.

10

DATING AND GENDER ROLES

Even though I've spent so much of my adulthood single, and so many of my attempts at romance have failed, I still don't feel called to a lifetime of celibacy. Earlier, in my twenties, I wanted God to let me off the hook and clearly call me into vocational singleness, but he never has. And I have given him so many chances to! But as I've moved on from my shame about wanting to be married, I realized that maybe I could embrace that desire a little more.

I wanted to try dating, to make time for it. Like I said, I had lots of opportunities for romance, but nothing really stuck—lots of shooting my shot and being let down. As romantic as I am—as good at matchmaking, as sociable and charming—I felt that things more important than dating deserved my time, attention, and energy. Plus, spending my twenties on campus with undergrads all day, and sometimes late into the night, wasn't the greatest place to meet a suitable suitor.

When my sabbatical rolled around, I decided to give myself a challenge: go on ten dates. I finally had a ton of time and energy, and what else was I going to do? A project, if you will. Give myself six months to find a boyfriend and potential husband. And then I'd get back to work! Because who has time for dating when you're doing the Lord's work?

When I started dating, a few things happened:

My dates were super nice but not for me.

I had feelings for a guy friend, but he didn't like me back.

And then, coronavirus.

Right when I had six months at my disposal, my first-ever global pandemic hit. Look, I'm not fooled into thinking that life and the world revolve around me but *come on*. Is that not a total sign from the heavens? I go on two dates and then the *entire world is ordered to go inside.*

I'm not saying the pandemic was my fault, but I'm also not saying I had *nothing* to do with it.

I have always looked at my life as a sitcom. The hijinks God and I get up to when it comes to my love life just feel unreal. Every guy I've ever liked? Doesn't wanna date me. Give myself some time to date? Jk. Go to your room, Bridget.

It's comedic, really.

TAKE A CHANCE ON ME

My dating journey had me facing a couple topics that I had been putting off for a while.

Gender roles, for example: Is it necessary for a woman to wait for the guy to make the first move? Obviously, my actions speak to where I stand on the answer to that question. I don't subscribe to traditional gender roles, but I've always been stuck wondering whether there might be something I don't know. Is there something innate about male–female relationships that makes them click, makes them work? I've been rejected every time; is it because I'm doing this wrong? I always tell my students that rejection builds character. It humbles you and helps you re-center your heart and ask where true validation comes from. (Jesus, duh.)

My character gets built at least once a year.

But I also feel like I've been rejected inside the church too. I put myself out there, offer myself and my giftings, and time and time again I have been let down.

I'm a strong, independent, outspoken woman, if you couldn't tell. What's more, I've held spiritual leadership positions and led in Christian community my entire adult life; but because I'm single, the churches I've attended don't know what to do with me. If I were married, a pastor might recognize my leadership and ask me and my husband if we could lead a small group or outreach, or maybe even an evangelism training. But when I've approached church leadership to offer those things, in which I am highly skilled and passionate, it's often met with hesitancy, skepticism, and distrust.

And then, when single men in the church get to know me, it seems that I intimidate them. They are taught that when they get married, they will be the head of their household and their wife will submit to them—but I just don't throw off those vibes, you know?

I'm loud. I'm an extrovert. I take up space. I'm a natural leader. I care about justice and good discipleship. I'm uninterested in helping in kids' church, with women's ministry, or in the kitchen. I want to see my peers grow closer to God and his heart. I want to help them learn how to share their faith in their lives and with their words. These are the things I'm passionate about, but we are not often given such a robust picture of what a woman can be in the kingdom of God.

I like that Proverbs 31 woman; I think she is so legit. But oh my gosh, that is not the woman the church has been asking me to be. They stop their ask at "a wife"—two words into the poem.

A wife of noble character who can find?
    She is worth far more than rubies.
Her husband has full confidence in her
    and lacks nothing of value.
She brings him good, not harm,
    all the days of her life. (Proverbs 31:10-12)

But I am not a wife.

Can I not be worth far more than rubies to the church?

Can I not bring the church good, not harm, all the days of my life?

Can I not work and use my skills and giftings and make decisions on behalf of and for the good of my church family?

Can I not be trusted to invest my life for the fruit of the church?

Can I not extend myself to the poor and the needy?

Of course I can.

This experience has gone on for so long. My leaders have this great opportunity to demonstrate trust and faith in who God made me to be as a gift to the church, but I am being underutilized because I am not married. I don't get to love and serve the church in a way that honors who I am. And I think it's because of fear.

So I'm stuck waiting for a chance to be taken on me as a leader—*and as a wife.* Why did God make me so lovable and sociable and romantic, and yet here I am so lonely? Why did he give me this heart for commitment and service and yet it feels so one-sided everywhere I go? Why is it that I haven't been chosen yet? What is it about me that draws men into deep friendship, but never more? Why do they see me as unworthy to take a romantic risk? Are they afraid too?

It's easy to make up answers to these questions. But that isn't a tower I am going to stay trapped in anymore. The truth is, men in the church and in my life are missing out. This isn't a me problem.

This is a cultural problem. It bears repeating: for far too long, American evangelicalism has been offering an unimaginative picture of what it means to be a follower of Jesus. The message I've heard in church is reduced to a male–female binary that begs us all to fit into a category and become spouses and parents. The end of Proverbs 31 says,

> Charm is deceptive, and beauty is fleeting;
> but a woman who fears the LORD is to be praised.
> Honor her for all that her hands have done,
> and let her works bring her praise at the city gate.
> (Proverbs 31:30-31)

Do not let that be lost on you! *A woman.* Not a wife or mother. A woman who fears the Lord. It is so damaging to hear your entire life that all you have to offer is as a wife and mother. The messages to men are even more damaging, and they impact the treatment of women. The picture we're given is that women are just to be helpmates to men, which shapes the desire of what a man is looking for and expecting in a woman. It also centers his desires and needs, rather than creating a picture of a partnership of reciprocity.

This is the saddest part of Christian culture to me—where is the vision and space for single people? I'm not talking about a singles ministry. When I show up at church again and again, and the picture I'm offered still doesn't quite line up with what I see in Scripture, it gives me pause. I've had to consider if there is a place for me as a single woman in churches like these.

For now, instead of running, I've chosen to run headfirst into those relationships and conversations. I've been honest with my pastors that more trust needs to be built, and I desire for them to step up their discipleship of me and our partnership together. And even though they are listening, it seems that it's going to take time. I need God's grace, mercy, patience, and love as I wait. This is one of the ways I'm choosing to be imaginative about the way I engage in my church community. I could go to other churches to get what I want out of the church experience, but I want to see it through with my community.

As for men that I attempt to date, I'm as honest with them as I can be. I leave them with some of these harder questions to ponder about themselves and what they want, but I am trying my best to not to let it be my problem.

While I'm in this process, waiting for others to "rise and call (me) blessed" as a single woman and waiting for the smartest (and hopefully funniest) man alive to come my way, I'm engaging with God about it all.

What do I need to drop? What do I need to reconsider? How do I leave behind the cracked foundation that I've been taught my whole life? How do I say yes to who God made me to be while also trying to find love in this context? I haven't felt equipped for it; it hasn't seemed possible.

A HEALTHY FOUNDATION FOR DATING

American Christianity in the early 2000s was so busy trying to get us not to have sex that it forgot to teach us about healthy dating. Leaders were so focused on a laundry list of sexual don'ts that they didn't teach us how to be friends with one another, how to honor one another. The evangelical church sinned greatly against us young people with its hyper focus on gender roles.

Ultimately, it was dehumanizing. It had us create objects of each other. We were given lenses through which to view one another as potential mates instead of coheirs to the kingdom of God. This context sexualized every cross-gender interaction. I grieve the unhealthy and unsatisfying foundation that was laid for our identities and relationships with one another as young followers of Jesus.

All of this might have been the reason I hardly dated as a young person. I was far too serious about it all. But I also think there was a baseline of fear that existed throughout my romantic interactions. I didn't want to do it wrong, but I also didn't like what we were being taught. I think it felt easier to avoid it altogether.

There's also the dating narrative and example from secular culture to consider. It's one of entitlement and consumption, and it's not far off tonally from the narrative of the church. Pop culture centers individual expression and taking what you want, getting what you need at whatever cost. It tends to glorify poor coping mechanisms and to leave us without lessons on how to be good to one another.

So where do you go to figure out how to date well as a follower of Jesus? The Bible doesn't have a chapter on it since dating wasn't a concept until the last century.

More than a decade of college ministry kind of forced me to engage with a better way. Watching other people try their hand at dating, I have absorbed much wisdom. The dos and don'ts. The pain and the sorrow of dating, along with the joy and delight of it.

My revelations here may leave you unsatisfied if you're looking for a step-by-step on how to date as a Christian. There's too much to cover, and really, I want to create the space for you to work it out yourself. Dating can be a great demonstration of our faith in what it means to be human in the kingdom of God.

Ultimately, a healthy foundation for dating comes down to dignity and honor.

Consider how Paul exhorts the Philippians to unite together:

> Therefore if you have any encouragement from being united with Christ, if any comfort from his love, if any common sharing in the Spirit, if any tenderness and compassion, then make my joy complete by being like-minded, having the same love, being one in spirit and of one mind. Do nothing out of selfish ambition or vain conceit. Rather, in humility value others above your-selves, not looking to your own interests but each of you to the interests of the others.
>
> In your relationships with one another, have the same mindset as Christ Jesus:
>
> Who, being in very nature God,
>   did not consider equality with God something to be
>   used to his own advantage;
> rather, he made himself nothing
>   by taking the very nature of a servant,
>   being made in human likeness.
> And being found in appearance as a man,
>   he humbled himself
>   by becoming obedient to death—
>   even death on a cross!
> Therefore God exalted him to the highest place
>   and gave him the name that is above every name,
>   that at the name of Jesus every knee should bow,
>   in heaven and on earth and under the earth,

and every tongue acknowledge that Jesus Christ is Lord,
to the glory of God the Father. (Philippians 2:1-11)

As followers of The Way of Jesus, we are invited to get on the same page as one another. To unite under his love and value each other above ourselves. Not to take advantage of each other, use each other, objectify one another, or oppress each other. We are called to a radical unity because of our connection to Jesus.

Paul's exhortation for us is to "have the same mindset as Christ Jesus" *in our relationships with one another.* Jesus, who had no reason to consider himself less than anyone, humbled himself to the lowest degree so that we may come close to God. And the result? Jesus was exalted as Lord to the glory of God the Father!

Can't the same invitation apply to our romantic endeavors? What holds you back from flipping the script of your dating life? I know we hardly look at it this way, but it's a chance for God's glory to shine through your humility with the person you're dating. How can you look to their interests rather than your own in your "common sharing in the Spirit"? If both parties are always looking to the interests of the other, no doubt they will be able to honor and dignify each other in their dating lives, no matter the outcome.

As followers of Jesus, we believe that literally every person is made in the image of the Divine. So, we need to act accordingly. Every interaction, every relational risk, every hard conversation, every time you shoot your shot is a chance to practice your belief that you and others are made divinely.

You are infinitely valuable and precious. So, when you are rejected or ghosted, you can practice remembering that you are loved and chosen. And you can extend grace and boundaries to the person who let you down. You can practice forgiveness, because ultimately, they are not accountable to you. God has that handled.

Those you date are also made of the Divine and are deeply human. They will make mistakes, but they too deserve honor and kindness. We can practice love in every romantic inter-action because it's a risk every time—it might have the best payoff, or it might totally tank. You are not entitled to a certain outcome. You are invited to keep choosing love and trust.

Dating is a chance to learn to communicate with grace, be brave in your honesty, speak the truth in love, and coura-geously set boundaries that will honor you and others. Dating can also be a great place to learn about yourself. What kind of people make good partners for you? What kind of people in-spire you to grow closer to the Lord and to the person you were made to be?

All these truths can apply to friendship as well, so what's the difference?

I think it's intimacy. Sometimes there are people we just connect with more easily, make us happy to be alive, and make us feel more like ourselves. There are special people with whom we feel safe to go deeper and with whom we want to share our time and emotions.

A way to honor and dignify others is to know that dif-ference. Sometimes, even in Christian community, we can use each other for emotional and physical intimacy without any kind of intentionality or commitment. That's a costly way to get what we want and need. Lack of intention and com-mitment can lead to dead ends and broken trust. It shouldn't be that way among us. Even if it feels costlier to lay good boundaries, it's worth it to step out of our habit of objectifying one another.

If we want to find love, we need to be willing to take risks on ourselves and one another. For some, those risks pay off quickly and beautifully. And for others like me, it may take a lot of time, but there are still many rewards to be had in the process. Lessons to learn. Self-awareness to grow in. Fun stories along the way. Growth in my character again and again. The journey of life.

Let your venture into dating be a chance to let God peel back another tentacle of your Octopus of Brokenness. He wants to bring you freedom, growth, and lots of love. He wants to help you grasp more clearly the relationship between your own humanity and divinity and in turn be found swimming in his grace.

As we step more fully into this life and intentionality with God and others, we can become better partners for each other in the family of God. As we de-center fitting everyone into a certain role and producing the same outcomes for everyone, we will be able to create space in the church for people to thrive as they are, no matter who or whose they become.

Pilgrimage Moment: Beholding One Another

As pilgrims on a journey together, we hold this space for each other: no one is better than anyone else, but instead we are all inherently valuable and beautiful, and we are on our own journeys. We don't ask each other to have a quicker or slower pace, and we don't ask each other to change our reason for being there in the first place. We learn to accept and create space for one another.

There is a contemplative concept called "beholding" that entails gazing upon a work of art or something in nature and soaking in its inherent worth without trying to judge it or apply outside value to it. When you behold something, you don't measure it up to anything else. You let it stand alone.

We can practice beholding one another.

Here's an idea: get in front of a mirror and stare at yourself for a while. As all the normal judgments rise to the surface of your thoughts, gently let them go and just keep soaking in your image. Look at all the shapes that make up your face and hair. What are the textures you see? How does the light fall on you? What colors do you notice?

What emotions arise in you? Do you naturally recognize your inherent worth outside the judgments and value systems you're used to? Are you able to behold your own dignity with a pure and unconditional love like God does?

Now apply that same kind of beholding to the people in your life. Can you behold their inherent dignity outside of who you think they should be or what you wish they would do? Practice beholding the people in your life in the small, in-between moments. Or ask their permission to behold them for a few minutes, even if it's uncomfortable. As you grow in your ability to behold others, your love for them will grow purer and more like God's love for them.

11

THE VIRGIN ONE SPEAKS

"Sex is like food."

Oh boy, I thought as I braced myself for this stranger's next words.

"If you go to a restaurant that you've never been to before and order something but don't like it, you won't finish the dish and you will hardly think of returning to that restaurant ever again," he said.

I was on a virtual Bumble date with a man who had just found out that I was a virgin.

I didn't ask him to, but he felt the need to tell me why he thinks sex before marriage makes sense. I had just met him thirty minutes before and his first words to me were, "You're so beautiful."

Thank you, but you hardly know me, I thought.

Before long, I could sense his character from his words and his story.

His attitude about sex felt objectifying to me. If sex is like food, you're saying our bodies are restaurants—created for a customer to show up, order what they want, hopefully like it, pay, and leave. If the service is good, they tip more than fifteen percent. This analogy broke down so fast.

I've never had sex. But I know that my body and other people's bodies aren't solely made to service each other's needs and pleasures. Sex *is* like food in that your body wants it and delights in it, but it's not like food because it can survive without it for long periods of time. I am not a dish to be served on a platter to a man, and that's why I did not give that man any more of my time after that phone call.

But I could hear the hurt in his story too. It made sense to me why he landed at such a view of sex. He felt entitled because so much had been chosen for him most of his life. And affection had been withheld from him in a previous relationship, so he wanted a freer love.

Everyone has reasons for their sexual ethic, good or bad.

People are all over the spectrum when it comes to beliefs and attitudes about sex and sexuality. Some display their sexuality for all the world to see and enjoy. And there are others who will never talk about any of this stuff. Although this topic is deeply personal, there's room in our current cultural climate to open up the conversation.

My whole life, I've had people tell me *lots* of things about sex and sexuality. And I've always been curious. Part of the reason is that I saw many representations of sexuality around me. My parents had become Christians after I was born; they were navigating the best ways to teach us about sex amid 1990s American Christianity. Which was *rough*, let me tell you.

We've been visiting many mountaintop experiences on this pilgrimage together, so let's talk about the highest one of all: the orgasm.

Okay, I'm only kidding.

Let's face it, though. We really do chase the high of physical pleasure, some of us more than others, and so much of pop culture revolves around sex. It sells. It keeps us hooked for seasons of television storylines. It's hot. It's controversial. It's private, it's public. It's taboo to talk about it, but we need to be talking about it more.

In a recent small group meeting, a friend said, "Heaven will be incredibly sexual because God is incredibly sexual." My ears turned red when I heard him say this, but I wanted to hear more! He went on to elaborate how the triune God that we know and love is all about the intimacy, pleasure, vulnerability, and reproduction that sex is made of. Sex offers a picture of who God is.

No wonder we are obsessed with it as a society.

There's no end to the public debates surrounding everything sexual. We argue about who can have sex and when. We argue about appropriate sexual expression. While we take sexual abuse seriously, justice is rarely served. Sex can produce *whole new humans*, but we have different views on when a fertilized egg is considered human.

Sexually transmitted infections are taken very seriously. There's a battle between sex positivity and exploitation in the porn industry. The global sex industry is riddled with dark situations for all types of people.

And on top of all of that, sex is not simple. It's not always fireworks and orgasms. It's a multifaceted experience that seems to touch all levels: physical, emotional, mental, and spiritual.

There's this dichotomy with the sexual that produces so many questions in me. Do you ever wonder why God made our "private" parts also the place where we derive the most pleasure? Why did he combine reproduction and orgasm for men? Why does it seem that across the board, most people consider this area of the human body fragile, private, and tender?

The older I get, the more I feel led to travel down the rabbit trail of these questions. The world's sexual ethic is so unsatisfying, and the "purity culture" of Western evangelicalism didn't really do it for me either.

And I'm a virgin in my thirties. I long to be satisfied.

VIRGIN JUST BECAUSE?

Let me tell you why I'm a virgin.

First of all, I am a virgin just because that's how the cookie crumbled. I've hardly been in a situation where sex was an option. Did I mention that Brandon was not only the first person I kissed but the last as well? It's embarrassing to admit, but I haven't even kissed a guy in over a decade.

And I don't know why no one has ever tried.

Okay, I take that back because as I was trying to fulfill my goal of going on ten dates during my sabbatical, I went on a socially distanced boba tea date with a guy who made me laugh. After learning more about his background and trying something different by not giving away what a goody-two-shoes I am, he asked me if I felt like we should pursue something romantic. I was a little surprised by his directness, but I admitted that I thought we'd be better off as friends since we have different values. He was definitely the easiest guy to be around of all my dates thus far, but it wasn't a love match by any means.

Even still, as we sat sipping our drinks on the side of a grassy hill, he asked, "Would it be totally out of the question to ask for a kiss?"

I responded with a laugh, "Absolutely! It's coronavirus and you're new!" Not to mention, I had just told him we would be friends and nothing more. We laughed it off, and I was impressed at his audacity, but it was a no for me.

So, I guess I could have been kissed if I had really wanted to. And trust me, I want to kiss, make out, have sex, etc. You don't know longing until you've been where I am—untouched, tumbleweeds blowing over your body.

But when it comes down to it, I don't want it with just anyone. I may feel desperate and needy at times, but in my heart of hearts, I want all of it in the best context.

So, here's how I see it. God wants the best for us. I think he made sex so beautiful and special because it's a whisper of his love, divinity, excellence, and intimacy. But the best context for that sex is with someone who is already committed to a covenantal relationship with you. I think it's important to practice physical intimacy with someone with whom you're willing to have emotional intimacy as well. Someone with whom you're willing to work through the hard parts of sex. The times when it doesn't work. To not have sex but connect in other ways when sex is not an option that day.

I only want to have one person to get naked and afraid with. And then naked and excited with. And then maybe not even always completely naked. I will only allow one person to sweat all over me. To bump uglies with me because sometimes, it's *ugly*.

And yet, it's beautiful to allow someone that close, to connect your flesh and become one for a time.

A SEXUAL ETHIC ROOTED IN GOD

In the early 2000s they were having us marry our virginities, with rings that claimed TRUE LOVE WAITS. I never got one of these, nor did I desire one, but the idolatry of true love was not lost on me: true love, and true love alone, is worth sex.

It's just a bizarre idea.

I'm not talking about abstinence. It's the idea that "true love" would be the main motivator for teenagers to wait until marriage to have sex. *Are you kidding me?* Do you know how many times teenagers think they have found true love before they can even drive? It was clearly a misguided tactic.

When I set out to write this book about singleness, I resolved to not make it about preparing for a new season, or to call singleness a gift, or to talk about *waiting.* Singleness is not about waiting. Singleness is just your life. It's not a season more or less special than any other, it's just a reality. It bears repeating: our truest waiting lies in the expectation that Jesus will return and make all things new and good. In the meantime, we are all living in wait, making the most of this life given to us.

For me, so much of my singleness has been throwing off this cloak of "waiting" projected onto me during countless purity-culture narratives in my past. We think we have to wait until marriage for all the good things to start, not just sex.

God's invitation for me to turn on all my burners, to have a big feast of life, was not just for one season. He continues to remind me, as I get hyper-focused on one pot while ignoring others, to look around. There's a whole meal waiting for me! I don't have to wait for life, I must participate.

For so much of my adulthood, this was me: "Ah, no, I'll just be that person when I'm married. I'll wake up at the same time every day, work out, eat healthy, and have a great routine and robust community when I'm married."

Have you ever had that thought?

I don't know why I also thought my husband was going to be a built-in accountability partner and life coach. I mean, I'm not ruling it out, but still, my growth and progress is between me and the Lord!

Although I believe that we aren't meant to wait for marriage for *everything* good, I'm resolved to wait until marriage to have sex. But in this period of my life, being more present with my body, awake to my emotions, longings, and desires, I have still needed to straighten out my own sexual ethic. I need it to be free of the purity culture of my youth and more deeply rooted in God.

I am sexual. I want to have sex. My body wants it. More now than ever. And sometimes it groans for it without my consent. I try and tell it to hush, but it's my body. I am not always in control. What I am in control of, though, is what I do with those groans.

EMBODIMENT

Embodiment is somatic practice—letting your physical state speak to your internal states, whether mental, emotional, or spiritual.

As you might recall, when I was the most depressed and lonely, ignoring my emotional pain and bad patterns, my body began to show me signs of my inner sickness through physical ailments. Then, when I was on the Camino, it dawned on me that I'd never paid this much attention to my body before because I had never felt this much consistent pain throughout the day. Some of us are wholly unaware of our bodies. It's a privilege in some ways, and in others, it's an obstacle.

American Christianity seems to treat the body with disdain and disregard rather than with gentleness and care. Our flesh is often spoken of as the primary enemy, responsible for all our sin. My body always felt weaponized within the walls of a church, and I knew that wasn't right.

Women receive very limited and odd messaging around our bodies. We are told to cover up—and I think it means more than just our bra straps. Cover up our desires. Be a body to someday be used and consumed, but don't just be your own body. Don't own it and cherish it, care for it, and love it. Cover it, cover it, cover it. Don't use it to sin or to cause anyone to sin.

Those are the messages we hear.

We don't often hear

- Your body is good.
- Sex is good.
- Your sex drive can kick into high gear in your later baby-making years.
- You may be more hormonal and feel your sexual appetite increase at certain times of the month.
- It's possible that at times your body will just want sex, even if you didn't bring it up.

None of those realities include the shame that a lot of us are used to. Men may have more consistent conversations around their inherent sexuality, but those conversations typically center around shame and sin management. Their bodies are often spoken of as tools of sin, and that their desire for sex, though inherent, is broken. If there were more conversations around the sacredness of our bodies, we might not have all these issues.

Our bodies are made from sex, and they are made (typically) to want sex.

Jesus is God Incarnate; God embodied as human. It is central to the gospel that Jesus was a man with a body. It matters! If he didn't have a body, then our faith in his bodily resurrection is a moot point. His flesh mattered. Had it not been pierced for our transgressions or bruised for our iniquities, we would not have access to the God who brings us peace and healing (Isaiah 53:5). If Jesus' flesh mattered and meant something, then ours does too.

Paul encourages the Roman church, "Therefore, I urge you, brothers and sisters, in view of God's mercy, to offer your bodies as a living sacrifice, holy and pleasing to God—this is your true and proper worship" (Romans 12:1).

So what does it look like to offer my body as a living sacrifice? How do I worship God with my body? All these questions got me wondering, What if there is a holy sexual expression across human experience? How might God want me to be self-controlled here? Is it to listen to my body and seek ways to satisfy those longings on my own? Or is it to seek nonsexual ways to satisfy my body with equal energy?

Masturbation, for example, is not directly addressed in Scripture, and modern theologians are all over the map on it. Realizing this made me wonder if there were a precedent for it that could be holy—without sin or lust or objectification. Can you engage with your own sexuality without it being dishonoring to others? I think so. There must be a way to invite God into that; or maybe God was there all along!

I am resolved to invite God into my sexuality, or go and find him there. I don't have all the answers here because this is all so new to me. It's also not something that I want to be ashamed of. My body is my body. God gave it to me and I want to honor that well.

Sex is just one of the experiences of life. And it is so temporary. Our sex drives, our abilities, our stamina—all temporary. Another mercy from God. If it lasted forever, we may never see each other!

My theology of sex is still forming, even as someone who doesn't have sex. And I hope it will continue to form for the rest of my life; I always want to learn about the mysterious things.

WHAT IS THE INVITATION FOR US?

If I'm choosing to wait for the best context for sex with a partner, what does it look like to be celibate for an unknown amount of time? For some, it can turn them bitter and entitled. It can mean believing lies about our worth and value. That's idolatry. If you think anything apart from God is going to truly answer a deep longing in your soul, you have some idols, baby.

If God's invitation is to say no to cheaper versions of what he has for you, how do you deal in the interim? Being lonely and feeling unchosen can feel like torture.

Is God okay with our suffering? Yes and no. He allows it. He's not really the cause of it, though. Suffering happens because of brokenness.

All of this brings up the question: What do you think this is all about, anyway—your needs getting met?

In the beginning, God made us and everything in the world because it was good. He wanted us and made us to want him. He made us for each other too, for delight and satisfaction. But when we start to believe that the story centers around us and our own strength and authority and entitlement, we sin. We step into death.

Do you believe God is sovereign and merciful and has good for you?

Probably sometimes, when things go your way.

But how do you believe and act when things aren't going your way? And what happens when they don't go your way for a very, very long time?

Look, so much has gone my way! God gave me so many things I prayed for and wanted, even when I put too much hope in those things. He has been merciful to keep me single because he knows better than I do that his way of life is best for me. And I get to choose every day to trust that singleness and celibacy are the best life for me right now.

But I have not always coped well when things haven't gone my way. Let me address my sin.

It is when I put myself in the center of the story and I don't believe that God has good waiting for me that I sin. When I care more about my body's needs than I do about addressing them in a healthy way, I have objectified others by consuming porn. There are so many terrible implications of being a consumer of porn, and I'm not sure it's my call here to list them all. The point is, there isn't one healthy thing about it. Porn has been the cheap and easy way to get off for so many of us. And there's a narrative in culture right now that says that's okay. But there's an equally loud narrative that addresses its damaging aspects, and they aren't all religiously based. Porn can be psychologically harmful. It's a way to consume sex with complete control and no consideration for others. It lacks vulnerability. This is not the invitation for people in the kingdom of God.

What is the invitation for us?

Shouldn't Christians be talking about sex instead of stealing away in the dark of the night to watch it on our screens? We need to take away the stigma of an open conversation about sex and sexuality with single people. If Christians are split down the line about so much of sex and sexuality, then obviously there's a lot to consider and talk about. We can handle the tension of our disagreements.

Let's bring what's in the dark into the light!

Especially because I do college ministry, I long to have better answers and practices when it comes to teaching a holy sexual ethic. Sex is one of the biggest topics on my students' minds. Too many times I've seen students run and hide from Jesus and community because of their sexual experiences. They don't feel like coming around because of what they've done or what's been done to them. That's not how it should be in Christian community. On one hand, if having sex is isolating you and causing you to withdraw from your relationships and your community, is it really worth it? That doesn't sound like good sex, it sounds like costly sex. On the other hand, if you don't feel like there's space for you in Christian community because of your sexual past or present, the community needs to change. We have to learn how to foster community that doesn't run people out the door, but invites them back in over and over, no matter what choices they make or things they've experienced.

Maybe you've had sexual experiences that you wish weren't a part of your story. Maybe you had no choice in the matter. You didn't deserve that. God wants to go there with you and bring his healing and love. He wants to free you from any shame of the past. I am not very well-equipped to speak into sexual abuse, but I do know that even more than good sex, God wants healing and wholeness for us. We are never beyond repair.

The time is now to create space for all types of stories.

Tenderness toward the experiences of LGBTQ+ people is rare in the Christian spaces I've grown up in. A reason I feel so passionate about singleness is that I know that a lot of people feel it harder than I do, and they need champions and cheer-leaders. I hope if anything, my long-standing singleness affords me some authority to say that I stand with you in your suffering. I am right with you in the questioning and wrestling with God. Your anger toward the church is valid.

There's nothing wrong with our questions or emotions. There must be clear and open space in our churches for all types of single people. Otherwise, whole groups will never walk through the doors and experience community, hear the good news on a regular basis, or be encouraged and cared for. There must be space for the exploration of a holy sexual ethic across the line. There must be space for confession, healing, and freedom from shame.

Jesus has freedom for us. Is your sexual ethic true freedom? Maybe, maybe not. That's something you have to work out for yourself. But this even applies to married people, doesn't it? What you believe and the way you interact with sex matters so much. It impacts marriages. Lots of married people aren't experiencing God's best in their sex lives either.

I'll end on this note: Don't wait to have these conversations about sex and sexuality with trusted people in your life and your church community. Don't wait until it becomes personal or impacts someone you love. Choose to love others now by practicing presence with them in their experience of singleness. In doing this, we will honor each other's stories and humanity, and therefore honor God.

Pilgrimage Moment: Communal Lament

Most of these pilgrimage moments have been activities that you can do by yourself because ultimately a pilgrimage into holy aloneness is something you can choose on your own.

However, as we've come to the end of our contemplative practices, in the spirit of a higher call for the church to be a safer space for conversations around sex and sexuality, I invite you into communal lament. Throughout this book I've named many ways that the American evangelical church has fallen short for single people. I've spent many hours and days contemplating it, so now it's time for a little action.

Rev. Dr. Barbara Holmes from the Center for Action and Contemplation gives us a picture of practicing communal lament in crisis:

> Communal lament is important for several reasons. It wakes us up and, in doing so, makes us mindful of the pain of our neighbors, who no longer can go about business as usual when the women begin to wail. Their keening rattles both marrow and bone. Who can remain in a stupor with all of that yelling?! But lament is important for another reason: The collective wail reminds us that we are not alone. The sheer power and resonance of a grief-stricken chorus reminds us that we are beings of quantum potential. We still have agency in every cell of our being, enough to survive—even this![1]

For those of us who have been on this journey together, let us be the grief-stricken chorus that reminds each other that we are not alone!

I'll begin our lament.

Lord, we cry out in repentance for the ways the Western evangelical church has weaponized bodies and closed doors on so many because of their experiences and realities with sex and sexuality. We lament the abuse that has gone on within the church's walls. We decry the ways we have been agents of shame and not agents of healing and peace.

God, I lament the ways that singleness has been a desolate and unhopeful place for many who belong(ed) to the church. I lament the ways that all types of singles have been alone, abandoned, and forgotten because of the ways they didn't fit into the narrow slots they were offered by unimaginative churches.

We are so sorry and so sad, God. It should not be this way among us.

Jesus, we cry out for a new way, for your resurrection life to come into all these dead places. We ask for the justice that only you can bring. Let there be a new day for us. Amen.

Feel free to sit in this moment a little longer and add your own lament. If you're having dissonance over this pilgrimage moment, linger there. What's going on inside of you? Is there something that stops you from stepping into lament?

Or perhaps you've been in lament for a while now, waiting for the wailing to grow louder. Well, we're here now. You're not alone.

12

YOU CAN DO IT

Elías Valiña was the priest of the church in O'Cebreiro (pronounced "Oh-Say-Bray-Ro"), a small town at the top of a mountain in Galicia, Spain; he is responsible for the restoration of the Camino de Santiago. Valiña died at the age of sixty in the year I was born, having been single his entire life. He honored the past by spending the last couple decades of his life bringing the Camino alive.

Valiña believed in the transformative nature of pilgrimage. His mission was to make the path more clearly visible, which led to a resurgence of pilgrims taking the Spanish journey. This man singlehandedly convinced the world to come on The Way of St. James, one that brings so much life and boosts the economy of northern Spain, a pilgrimage rooted in history and religion.

Valiña's nephew speaks of the Camino and his uncle's legacy in this way,

> This is the daily tonic. People arriving from all over the world, who share their dreams along with their sorrows. The Camino allows you to travel to a hidden village in the mountains of Lugo and, at the same time, be at the centre of the world. There is no greater university than this, as long as you are open to listen.[1]

It was because of Valiña that I was able to learn one of my life's most important lessons. From the beginning of my trip to Spain, I had heard about the hike to O'Cebreiro. Nick wasn't sure which day of the hike it was; he kept telling me that there was a crazy hike up a mountain, and he kept thinking it was the next day or the next, but it took more than a week into my journey for us to get there. Every day I braced myself for a painful situation: a thirteen-mile hike leading to a mountain, where people often took a horseback ride an additional five miles to the tiny town at the top.

It was about a week into my walk, and it was a gorgeous day, but like I said before, I had quickly learned my mental limit. Thirteen miles is beyond when my feet ache, my body asks, "Why?" and I just get irritable. I ran out of mental stamina, so I was looking forward to my horseback ride. The only problem was, when I got to the little town at the base of the mountain, there were no more horses available that day. It was about 1:30 p.m., I hadn't eaten lunch, and the businessman told me his horses needed to rest. *I* needed to rest.

But it was Roshelle's birthday. We were all meeting up that night to have dinner together to celebrate. I had no other choice, and it's what I wanted. I wanted to be there with my friends laughing, eating, celebrating life. So, I walked into the last restaurant on the way out of town, ordered ravioli, and was joined by a new friend I had made only a few days before. (He slept in our fancy albergue room snoring through the night on the bunk below me. But I don't blame him, he was at least sixty-five years old and was doing the Camino on his own.) He had decided to stay in the town that night and happily watched me prepare for my trek up the mountain.

As I ate, he told me about why he was on the Camino. He kept calling himself a "true atheist," but he wanted to see if going on this journey would act as some kind of Catholic karma for his family. His daughter, who was a mother of two, was fighting cancer. He wanted with all his heart to take her place. He cried as he told me about his family back in the States. I told him that although he was a true atheist, I found his character to be quite like God's.

So many times, as a single woman, I have found myself in precarious situations like that—the audience of an emotional man or a drunk adult needing a mother. I'm not about to make a statement that we women get to be mothers whether or not we have children. No, I just think the world needs spiritual sisters and mothers to comfort, exhort, and encourage. Sisters can be a gift.

That moment captured so many of the ways that I had grown into Woman of God Bridget. Even though I was out of luck for a horse that afternoon, and I was annoyed and tired, I decided to take a beat and collect myself before doing the next hard thing. My friend had awkwardly dawdled in the restaurant, so I invited him to sit and watch me eat. A very odd scenario, not one I would normally invite or experience back home. And then I listened well, with my mouth full of pasta. I let this grown human share his story and cry.

Ultimately, I didn't let all these weird and hard scenarios derail me. I didn't let another person's story sink into my soul and take over my thoughts or emotions like I would have in the past. I let him be him, and I let me be me. And I had to get going.

So with that, I headed up the mountain. Given my love/hate relationship with hiking, it took a lot of grit and tenacity and lots and lots of breaks—look, I'm not a mountain goat! But sure enough, I climbed that gorgeous mountain through terrain made of my childhood dreams. At one point, a man came down the path on a horse, with another trailing behind. It had to be one of the most comedic moments of my life. The thing I wanted (an available horse) was right in front of me, but it was too late. They were headed down the way I came. There was no way I could convince them to turn back around and take me all the way up to O'Cebreiro. I didn't even try.

As I climbed, I realized that I was making okay time. I had come to understand my pace, and even gave myself a little leeway when I reported my ETA to Nick. Then two brilliant things happened.

First, I got near the summit of the mountain range. I was up so high that I could see for miles and miles and I was amazed. I felt elated that I made it that far in just a few days. All the mountains I could see were those that I had hiked through! My body brought me that far. My little muscular body. My exercise-induced-asthma-ridden body! I couldn't believe it.

Secondly, I crossed over into Galicia, the final province of the trek, which is basically known as Irish Spain. My people. Suddenly, the words on all the signs were in Gaelic-style manuscript letters. Something deep in my soul resonated with these people who might have shared ancestry with me. My day was turned around completely. Serotonin pulsed through my body. I was so happy. It's weird to think of my bad attitude the first part of the day—the majority of my journey.

Here came another mountaintop moment, alone with the Lord speaking the same old truths to my heart. This time, I was hearing that I could do it. I was capable of climbing all the mountains life had for me. I, Bridget Patricia Catherine Gee, was made for this. I didn't need to be a mountain goat. I didn't need to be further along in life. I didn't need to be another person. I had made it there by the grace of God and because of the strength he had given me. I spent so many of the first thirteen miles that day just wishing and praying for there to be a horse for me to take to the top. But there wasn't, and I went on anyway.

If that's not a metaphor for my single life, then I don't know what is!

Nearly four years had passed since my fit with God on the climb up to the Great Wall. And he was faithful to bring me through even more. Look who I had become! I was so proud of myself for climbing a mountain after spending all day hoping I wouldn't have to. I was so amazed at who God made me to be. I was rejuvenated there at the top. I had more energy in the last two miles than I'd had all day long.

What if that's the story for my singleness?

What if I've spent more than half my life wishing and hoping that I wouldn't have to make the climb alone? What if I have been praying all my life for God to send someone to help carry me along, support me, do the hard work with me, only to find out there's no husband for me all this time?

If that day on the journey is symbolic, then what I can take from it is that I will be okay! What I told God on Catalina Island was true: if he never sends me a horse, I mean, a spouse, then nothing. Nothing changes!

When the moment comes to set out on an even more daunting journey than I've already experienced, then I need to take a beat and gather myself. I need to slow down and get what I need so I can move forward, to put one step in front of the other, and to keep saying yes.

We can take the easy options. We can ride horses or call taxis to take us where we need to go. Sometimes we need to do that. And as we pilgrims say, "Everyone has their own Camino." But I think when the options are laid out, it's clear which one God has for you. For me so far, that's been singleness.

Wow, my singleness really has been that metaphor of a difficult climb that never seems to end. And God has been faithful to show me again and again and again that he has me, and that he made me well, and that I can trust him.

I've had many reasons why my trust in him has wavered:

- I have believed many lies about my lovability.
- I've been let down and hurt many times.
- He made me to want something that has never been mine.
- I've treated him like a genie, as if we made a deal of some sort that he would grant my wishes in exchange for my utter devotion.

Thank God that he's helped me see the truth through it all. Thank God that he's helped me out of those patterns and wrong beliefs. Thank God that he's given me strength to live in the tension of the unknown in my life.

Here's the thing though: the climb and doing it alone—it isn't all bad. In fact, it can be really satisfying. It can be beautiful. It can be hilarious. It makes you stronger. It makes you realize what you're capable of. I feel like I'm writing a Miley Cyrus song circa 2009.

I am so grateful that this is the life God has had for me thus far. I am humbled to have had all these opportunities and experiences during my singleness. God has romanced me, he has provided robust community. He has been faithful to peel back the tentacles of my Octopus of Brokenness and restore relationships in my life. He's met me on mountains all over the world to tell me the truth when I'm tempted to forget. He's been with me in the depths of my sadness and loneliness and graciously pulled me out of it. He's helped me see who he made me to be and learn to embrace her fully. He gave me a new way of embodying my faith: being present, creating space for myself and him. He's developed my perspective on how to love and honor others and myself along the way. He challenges the anti-kingdom values I've learned and helps me live as a true coheir of his kingdom.

What a mercy to have lived this life as a single person!

Just because I don't have it all doesn't mean I don't have anything. I actually have most things. I have learned gratitude for what I do have and will practice that for as long as it's mine.

My friends were waiting for me at the end of the path into O'Cebreiro (which looks like what I imagined Hogsmeade in Harry Potter would look like). They celebrated with me as I crossed the finish line. And it was dusk, the most beautiful time of day. Many people sat on that part of the mountaintop town to look out on all the mountain ranges, probably reflecting on how their bodies brought them that far, like I had earlier in the afternoon.

Hear from me the lesson I learned that day: You can do it!

So many of the things in life that we don't want to do, that are hard, can still be worth it in the kingdom of God. And things can change so quickly.

That day that I got to the summit, I recorded a video and said, "May I never do this again," as a half joke and half prayer. But for some reason a couple days later I was completely changed. A little seed started to sprout in my heart to someday bring students with me on the Camino.

Returning home from Spain, I knew what my life would look like, but I didn't really know what I was in for. I finished my last semester at UA on staff, and I only kind of stumbled over the finish line of 2019. I started to learn to not take on people's problems as my own, draw better boundaries, and pay attention to my own body. By the time I went on sabbatical, I was so ready for a new setting, with friends new and old, taking new risks. And then the pandemic happened.

During this time, my dad was diagnosed with mild cognitive impairment, which means that in a few years, he could have full-blown Alzheimer's.

Life happens. There may not be a horse for you today. Your spouse might never meet your father and vice versa. You might've thought that 2020 was the year you'd finally meet your husband, and then the world goes into lockdown.

We are not in control of the future and what happens there. There are some things we can have some control over, some things we can plan for. Most of the time, you just have to put one foot in front of the other, accept who you are and where you are and keep going. Sometimes you will feel on top of the world and realize how far you've come. Sometimes you'll sit on a rock and watch what you want pass you by.

Life just is hard! We are meant for a better world. All the good stuff of life is just a taste of what is to come. You aren't there yet. Your answer is on its way.

So come quickly, Lord! May my life be a testimony of my longing for you—the best thing, far more than I long for anything else.

The same week I found out this book was going to be published was the same week I got a new position with

InterVarsity—as the spiritual formation coordinator for our national Study Abroad team. Essentially, I'm the director of our European pilgrimages. Now it's my job to take people on the Camino and other pilgrimages like it. God did change my life after all because I said yes to being alone with him. As I continue to say yes to a life with him that includes me being single, things seem to just get better and better—whether it's that my risks seem to reap wonderful rewards or that the seasons of loneliness draw me into deeper intimacy with him. As time goes on, I recognize more and more that life with Jesus is the sweetest thing.

Jesus said it himself:

> The kingdom of heaven is like treasure hidden in a field. When a man found it, he hid it again, and then in his joy went and sold all he had and bought that field.
>
> Again, the kingdom of heaven is like a merchant looking for fine pearls. When he found one of great value, he went away and sold everything he had and bought it. (Matthew 13:44-46)

Could it be God's infinite mercy that I'm still single?

Something has truly changed in me. At one time I was seeking love in all the wrong places; now I am growing into a tree planted beside streams of living water (Psalm 1:3, Jeremiah 17:7-8). I know what my shepherd has for me: that I would never be wanting (Psalm 23:1-2), that I would be safe and strong and loved and fully alive no matter what (John 4).

Who am I to say that marriage is the treasure worth my life? Without it, I have still learned the lessons I know my friends are learning in marriage. I know death to self. I know and continue to work on communication. I know patience—and impatience. I know the humility of apologizing when you're wrong.

I know the hard choice of forgiving someone you love who hurt you.

I am not lacking as a single person.

I believe more and more that my life is exactly what it is supposed to be. I've learned to receive God's grace and love, to love myself, and to be loved by others. I don't have to wait for the fullness of what life has to offer! I have the great privilege of being sold on that which is really life: death to self and resurrection life in Christ. I am living proof that Jesus and his invitations are more than enough, and I will never believe otherwise—even if I do find myself married someday.

Friends, you too have a choice to believe with me. Will you choose our Father with me again and again every day? Will you do the work to believe that he is worth your life laid down, at the foot of the cross—a symbol of his great love for you— letting his resurrection power lift you into the life that is truly life?

No longer wait for something so simple as romantic love to come along. Run wildly after the One who chose you long ago and choses you every day.

"You will seek me and find me, if you seek me with all of your heart. I will be found by you, declares the Lord" (Jeremiah 29:13-14).

To find God is the best thing.

What are you waiting for?

Acknowledgments

I want to start by thanking Rod Pauls for telling me to submit a proposal to lead a seminar at InterVarsity's National Staff Conference in 2017. I had been on staff for four and a half years and the powers that be let me and Michael Gehrling colead a seminar called "Singleness in Mission." It hardly had anything to do with mission, and in true Bridget fashion, I created a listening prayer activity for all of us to do. I thank Rebecca Carhart for attending that seminar and approaching me afterward to ask if I had considered writing a book about singleness. I had. But I wasn't ready to be the Singleness Gal yet.

Thanks to Al Hsu for talking through what the proposal and publishing process looked like, and then waiting for me to get my guts up to actually write the book. It took me starting a podcast and nearly four years to make it finally happen. Your coaching, advocacy, and willingness to hold space for me has been vital to this process.

Thank you to Courtney Clapp, my gal pal who has seen me through it all. You coached me in getting my very first ugly draft done, and you've been the best cheerleader and hype lady a girl could ask for. This book wouldn't exist without your support.

Thank you to Felicia, Dom, Ivanna, and Kathryn, who have heard all these stories ad nauseum, but were still right there to help me process, brainstorm, and panic a little over sharing my life with an audience of strangers.

Thank you to all my friends who read the absolute worst draft of this book and gave me valuable feedback. You know who you are, and you will be the only ones who get to hear me sing that much of Rapunzel's opening number.

For everyone whose name is mentioned in this book—thank you. You are in my story because you mean the world to me. Thank you for being a part of my pilgrimage into holy aloneness. You are a part of why I know God more deeply and why I've been strong enough to share my story with others.

And to my mom—thank you for being the best. You are the greatest example of love I have ever received; you have championed me in my singleness the most, all while holding a healthy dose of hope that I would find a man that meets your expectations. Your words of encouragement and wisdom have stayed in my heart this entire time, and I finally did it. I wrote the book!

Notes

2. THE MOST ROMANTIC ONE

[1]Robert Farrar Capon, *The Supper of the Lamb* (Garden City, NY: The Modern Library, 2002), 189.

3. COMMUNITY PART ONE: WHEN YOU HAVE IT

[1]Henri J. M. Nouwen, "January 7: The Gift of Friendship" in *Bread for the Journey* (San Francisco: HarperSanFrancisco, 1997).
[2]Curt Thompson, *The Soul of Desire* (Downers Grove, IL: InterVarsity Press, 2021), 42.

6. LONELINESS

[1]"The History of Women and Banking Thanks To RBG," Flagship Bank, September 20, 2020, www.flagshipbanks.com/blog /the-history-of-women-and-banking-thanks-to-rbg.
[2]Rebecca Traister, *All the Single Ladies: Unmarried Women and the Rise of an Independent Nation* (New York: Simon and Schuster, 2016), 83.

7. LETTING GO

[1]Curt Thompson, *The Soul of Desire* (Downers Grove, IL: InterVarsity Press, 2021), 143.

8. EMBRACING MY AUTHENTIC SELF

[1]Ian Morgan Cron and Suzanne Stabile, *The Road Back to You: An Enneagram Journey to Self-Discovery* (Downers Grove, IL: InterVarsity Press, 2016).

9. HOLY ALONENESS

[1]"Understanding Desert Monasticism," Northumbria Community, www.northumbriacommunity.org/articles/understanding -desert-monasticism.

11. THE VIRGIN ONE SPEAKS

[1]"Crisis Contemplation: Communal Lament," The Center for Action and Contemplation, July 28, 2021, https://cac.org/daily-meditations/communal-lament-2021-07-28/.

12. YOU CAN DO IT

[1]"O'Cebreiro, the Town of the Camino," El Camino con Correros, February 11, 2017, www.elcaminoconcorreos.com/en/blog/o-cebreiro-the-town-of-the-camino.